'This well-researched book will tell you things that you will probably not have known about Christchurch and its history. Of interest to visitors to the town as well as residents who may want to explore parts of the borough they don't get to see very often. Dip into any part of this book to find a fascinating fact that will whet your appetite to know more about the town and some of its more colourful historical figures.'

Allan Wood, Communications Officer,
Christchurch and East Dorset Councils

'The Christchurch we know today is one of the most beautiful towns in England and was proudly taken over by Dorset in the county boundary changes.'

Harry Ashley,
Explore Dorset

*Jonathan Sells' vision in stone
in the garden near Place Mill.*

Lesser Known
Christchurch

Steve Roberts

Roving
Press

© 2015 Steve Roberts

Published by Roving Press Ltd
4 Southover Cottages, Frampton, Dorset, DT2 9NQ, UK
Tel: +44 (0)1300 321531
www.rovingpress.co.uk

First published 2015 by Roving Press Ltd.

ISBN: 978-1-906651-268

British Library Cataloguing in Publication Data
A catalogue record for this book is available from the British Library.

Cover design by Tim Musk.
Back cover photographs: Edwardian holidaymakers c. 1900 and Sea Vixen ©
Hampshire County Council. Provided by Hampshire Cultural Trust; old trolley bus
courtesy of Christchurch Electricity Museum; 'Sam' photograph by Ross Whitehair.

Set in 11.5/13 pt by Beamreach (www.beamreachuk.co.uk).
Printed and bound by Beamreach Printing (www.beamreachuk.co.uk).

Contents

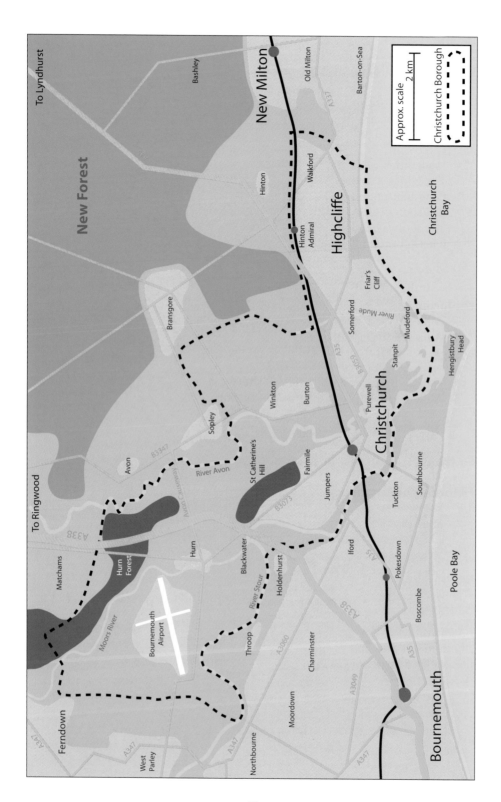

Preface

This book is part of a series of *Lesser Known* guides published by Roving Press that look at Dorset towns. I was thrilled to be asked to write this particular book, as I live in Christchurch and love the place. What could be better than writing about the town you love? Having said that, I have tried to include the whole borough, as there is more to Christchurch than simply the historic town centre.

Christchurch is a place with many hidden treasures, nuggets of history and things to be discovered. It is a sad truism that we often overlook what is on our doorstep, so this book will appeal to residents who would like to know more about their town, and visitors. As well as descriptions of places, people and events that make Christchurch special, there are contributions from people who live and work here.

There are also six walks to help you explore for yourself. Many of the places mentioned in the text are highlighted in the walks and shown on the walking maps, which I hope will be a useful aid to discovering the town.

Steve Roberts

Acknowledgements

Thanks to everyone who contributed, including those who provided personal stories. The author is grateful to Mike Andrews of Christchurch History Society for critiquing the history section, Allan Wood of Christchurch Borough Council for proof-reading and supplying some of the photos, Mel Baldwin of Christchurch Borough Council who also provided photos, and Mike Beams for guided tours of the Priory. The author would also like to acknowledge the efforts of all those local historians who have gone before him, who made his life so much easier, including those at Christchurch History Society. Whilst many people were consulted in the writing of this book, any errors are the author's alone. Above all, thanks to the author's dear wife Val, who always maintained that he had a book in him. It looks like she was right.

Christchurch – where time is pleasant.
The Quomps at Town Quay
is a focal point for many events.

Introduction

One of the 19 or so blue plaques around the town.

Christchurch's human past dates to prehistoric times, antiquity trumpeted by a blue plaque on the north side of the by-pass on the way to the supermarket. The ground under the modern car park here was occupied in the past by Saxons and, before them, Iron Age, Bronze Age and, earliest of all, Neolithic peoples. Christchurch has much fascinating history, but there is more to it than old buildings, venerable tales and blue plaques. There must be something about it that attracts around 1.5 million visitors a year.

Some people dismiss it as a town for elderly people, as newspapers revelled in stories in 2013 that Christchurch had the highest proportion of retirees in the country (nearly 30% of its population of 47,750 were pensioners). It is fair to say though that Christchurch's seniors are active and enjoying a special microclimate, sheltered by the Isle of Wight, which may be one reason why life expectancy here is above the national average. Yet the town has much to interest and entertain younger people as well, and in researching this book the author was 'blown away' by the opportunities offered to youngsters.

Christchurch has much to commend it then, yet also has challenges ahead; a borough where it is confidently declared that 'Time is Pleasant' should move with the times but must also make the best of what it has – a tricky balancing act. The high

Christchurch in bloom.

street continues to do reasonably in a time when its death has been trumpeted nationally. There may not be as many independent retailers as was, yet there are still interesting shops, lively pubs, plenty of cafés and important facilities such as the Christchurch Information Centre, library and cinema/arts centre here. You need never tire of visiting Christchurch's historic centre.

However, nothing stands still forever and one of the most controversial schemes ahead could be Christchurch Borough and East Dorset District Councils' 'Core Strategy', which sets out the planning strategy to 2028 and could see around 1,000 new homes built on green belt in the borough. Some say green belt should be sacrosanct; others believe that to keep Christchurch and its high street viable we need younger people and therefore must build homes for them. Nowhere is 'timeless'. Christchurch may have a past, but it also has a future and, to safeguard that future, it must move with the times.

With this in mind much hard work goes on to ensure Christchurch continues to be a place people want to visit. As Christchurch Information Centre Manager Sara Stewart-Haddow says:

'Christchurch sits between the New Forest and Jurassic Coast but also has its own history, with the Priory, castle ruins, Saxon mill and Red House Museum. It is a good centre from which to explore the wider area, yet, in itself, has

everything for the walker and those who enjoy the coast, beaches and fishing, also offering a quieter environment for people to enjoy. Regular events such as the annual Food and Wine Festival, the Christchurch Music Festival and Stompin' on the Quomps bring people in. We have restaurants for all tastes and budgets, which have survived the test of time, and independent little shops. It really is a wonderful place, which has everything a tourist wants. We even have our own microclimate, so we often experience better weather than elsewhere. I believe Christchurch has an extremely bright future with lots to look forward to, especially with "staycation" now in vogue. When I moved here I couldn't believe how much it had to offer and still feel like I'm on holiday. Visitors often say they wish they could move here themselves. We are that lucky.'

Another thing setting Christchurch apart is its sense of community. Former WPC and Territorial Army officer Brenda Traylen is now a volunteer special constable.

'We have a small-town atmosphere, everyone knows one another and people say "hello". Courtesy is more prevalent than elsewhere. We get crime of course, everywhere does, but it is low-level. I loved dealing with the youngsters and tried to get a rapport with them; they still come up and speak to me. I set up the Safer

View from the Priory tower, with the High Street and St Catherine's hill in the distance.

Neighbourhood Team, which is dedicated to specific needs and policing priorities of the local community. Members of the public could bring problems, and the nature of these illustrated what a nice place this is to live. One example of the community spirit is the annual fish and chip supper for less mobile senior citizens, which sees a real coming together, with transport provided by the local Round Table, entertainment from Ivo the Clown and youngsters at the Lighthouse, funding from local retailers and presents donated by local people. I've been privileged to be involved with this the last 15 years.'

On Parley Road approaching the airport and entering the borough, this sign shows that Christchurch is not inward looking, being twinned with four other towns and cities around the globe.

Brenda's fundraising exploits are legendary and in 2004 she was awarded an MBE for services to the community (policing and charity). Volunteers help keep the borough ticking. Sandra Prudom from the Christchurch Community Partnership says:

'[The Community Partnership] works with other groups, addressing local needs, making best use of available expertise and resources, avoiding duplication and filling gaps where possible. We directly deliver some projects such as Christchurch Angels, Dial-a-Bus and Neighbour Cars. The quarterly Volunteer Forum is our public face where groups meet, discussing progress, and acts as a catalyst for new projects. Christchurch Angels, established over a year ago, with 30-odd volunteers, provides support to those in short-term need, which could, for example, keep someone out of hospital. Dial-a-Bus is a door-to-door service for anyone finding it difficult using public transport. We also worked with local churches, setting up a food bank in Christchurch, and with them are continuing to develop a project to furnish homes for folk emerging from crisis, such as domestic violence or homelessness. This is a great example of Partnership working using Dial-a-Bus and Christchurch Angels to collect and deliver furniture. I wouldn't want to live anywhere else as Christchurch is small enough to be a real community, where we can all work, as our CCP strapline says, to "build a better Christchurch together".'

A Brief History

Christchurch has a long and fascinating past which needs understanding before exploring and appreciating the town and its environs. Humans have been padding about here since the New Stone Age. Hengistbury Head promontory closes off one side of Christchurch Harbour, offering the town crucial protection from the ravages of the sea. Ancient peoples lived on the Head, as well as 'under' the municipal car park, and the Head became one of this country's most important trading ports. Hengistbury Head is not part of Christchurch, being across the water in Bournemouth, but it must be mentioned as it is part of Christchurch's story. Without it there would be no Christchurch, either past or present.

Christchurch was founded in Anglo-Saxon times in about AD 650. It is said that Birinus, a missionary of the pope, baptised the King of Wessex, then founded a Saxon church on the Priory site. The town later became one of Alfred the Great's fortified burghs, protecting against the Vikings. Christchurch's military pretentions were displayed early, built on (literally) in later times. Christchurch warrants a mention in the *Anglo-Saxon Chronicle*: 'Then Aethelwold … seized the manor at Wimborne and at Christchurch without the consent of the king and his councilors.' The year was AD 901 and the king was Edward, son of Alfred the Great. The first mention of a priest here is in AD 985 and his name was Sulfric.

Christchurch had a different name in those days: 'Tweoxneam' and then 'Twynham', as recorded in the *Domesday Book* in 1086. Both names mean 'between the rivers', which makes sense as the town sits betwixt the rivers Avon and Stour. Indeed, the local leisure centre is called Two Riversmeet. A Saxon mill (Place Mill) is on Town Quay and was listed in *Domesday*; there was also Knapp Mill (where the waterworks is today), Mead Mill (close to Knapp) and Town Mill (or Port Mill), which was on the Mill Stream, probably roughly opposite the modern ducking stool.

The Normans certainly left their mark, raising some of the town's most impressive structures, including the late-11th-century Priory and early-12th-century castle. The Priory is the stuff of legend. It was as though God himself had chosen this site. Attempts to build on nearby St Catherine's Hill were thwarted as building stone kept moving to the plain below. The Priory building site was then visited by a mysterious carpenter. His most telling contribution concerns the 'miraculous beam', cut too short, destined to be discarded, until the 'man with no name' somehow rectified this. The church (and hence town) was unsurprisingly named Christ's Church. The name rang true in 1990 when, in a violent storm, a tower pinnacle blew down; 380 kg of stone fell on the nave roof, making a large hole, before lodging on a roof truss

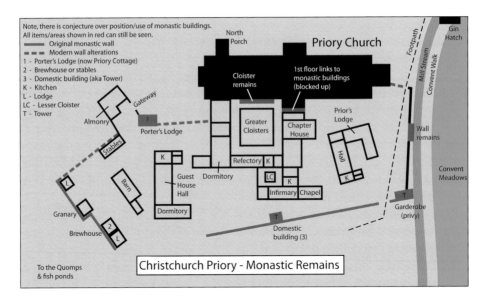

Note, there is conjecture over position/use of monastic buildings.
All items/areas shown in red can still be seen.
——— Original monastic wall
■ ■ ■ Modern wall alterations
1 - Porter's Lodge (now Priory Cottage)
2 - Brewhouse or stables
3 - Domestic building (aka Tower)
K - Kitchen
L - Lodge
LC - Lesser Cloister
T - Tower

Christchurch Priory - Monastic Remains

The miraculous beam inside the Priory at the east end, seen end-on within the small open arch.

The Priory viewed from the south side, where the Greater Cloisters and other monastic buildings would once have been.

which stopped its further descent. People sheltering in the Priory were saved by miraculous beam number two.

As well as the Priory itself, there are other leftovers from Christchurch's former monastic past, including walls, towers, the old Porter's Lodge and garderobe block (privy).

Unusually, Christchurch comprised three manors (districts). Most important was the honour (or lordship) of Christchurch ('honour' denoting extensive, by which the lord (often the king) granted subsidiary manors to others). Lesser manors were those of the Borough of Christchurch and Christchurch Twynham. Baldwin de Redvers received the burgh (which became the Manor of the Burgh, or Borough, of Christchurch) from Henry I, and de Redvers in turn granted lands to the canons of the partly built Priory, which became the Manor of Christchurch Twynham. The three manors have existed for a millennium and are still there, albeit their function today is almost entirely honorary.

Christchurch was first invited to send two members to parliament in 1308 but allegedly declined, being 'too poor'. The local economy must have improved by Elizabeth I's time (1571) when Christchurch first sent members regularly to parliament.

The castle meanwhile led a chequered existence, featuring in violent civil war (1135–54) between rival claimants to the throne, Stephen and Matilda, when Stephen's follower Walter de Pinkney seized it, only to be battle-axed to death in the churchyard. It hosted the Magna Carta barons in 1215, much to the chagrin of King John.

A plaque unveiled close to Constable's House in June 2015 commemorates the 800th anniversary of the Magna Carta and King John's stays in the town.

During the English Civil War (1642–51) it was slighted at the hands of Oliver Cromwell's forces. Christchurch, Royalist at the outset, changed hands during the war, after which the castle was besieged by Royalists in 1645, before Cromwell decided enough was enough and gave us today's ruin. Fighting must have been fierce, with cannon balls and shot found in the Mill Stream. The parish of Christchurch was considerably larger in those days, including much of modern Bournemouth (Iford, Throop, Holdenhurst and Muscliffe).

Christchurch Castle – built by the Normans, battered by Cromwell.

Given Christchurch's waterways, it is hardly surprising there are several bridges. The oldest is the medieval Grade II-listed Place Mill Bridge. There are three Grade I-listed bridges in the town centre: 15th-century Town Bridge and Mews Bridge, and early-19th-century Waterloo Bridge to the east which recalls the famous battle of that name.

Place Mill Bridge, with its Saxon arches.

After the Restoration (1660), Edward Hyde, Earl of Clarendon, bought the Lordship of the Manor of Christchurch in 1665 and tried to combat the problem of the harbour being inaccessible to larger ships by cutting a new entrance through part of Hengistbury Head. Thankfully his plans did not come to fruition as, had he damaged the Head, the town would most likely have been deluged by seawater.

The harbour may have been out of bounds to larger ships but that did not impede the fishing industry or illicit smuggling, which did a roaring trade. Christchurch, Stanpit and Mudeford are full of properties, particularly inns and former inns, that attracted smugglers. With customs cutters hindered by the difficult harbour entrance, the coast was clear for smugglers' activities, until 1784, when a confrontation led to the death of a Royal Navy officer and subsequent execution of a smuggler. Such was the infamous Battle of Mudeford. Christchurch's history has not always been serene.

The perfectly legal business of fusee chain manufacturing put the town on the map in the late 18th century. This involved creating intricate chains, key components of watches and clocks, business starting up at premises in the High Street in 1790 under Robert Cox's stewardship. Within 3 years Cox secured a monopoly on British production, making Christchurch the UK capital for fusee chain production. Girls as young as nine, many from the workhouse, were employed in the business, working up to 70 hours a week; time was not pleasant in Christchurch for all its citizens. In 1845 William

Hart, son of a Christchurch shoemaker, opened up his own factory in Bargates. This was almost certainly the last purpose-built fusee chain factory anywhere. Hart employed 104 women, children as young as 12 and two men (women's hands were better for this work). Time ran out on this business though; changes in the way clocks and watches were made ensured the town's period of pre-eminence lasted for just over a century.

Also in the late 18th century Christchurch was considered the first place in England for knit silk stockings (mainly for men!), as confirmed by the Universal British Directory (1792). Men wore them with breeches until trousers took over. Previously Christchurch had also been famous for the manufacture of frieze cloth, a coarse woollen, mainly used for overcoats. Later, in the 19th century, the town became a centre for taxidermy (fashionable with Victorians).

Hart's former fusee chain factory; at 22 m long by 5.5 m wide, its narrow width and large windows permitted maximum light for the intricate work.

Brewing was also an important local industry, with beer being one of the most significant exports from Town Quay. Prior to work starting on the town's sewerage in 1902, beer would have been a safer drink than water. In 1855 there were reputedly six breweries in the town. Bow House in the High Street is a reminder of Christchurch's brewing heritage (a remnant of Christchurch Brewery). The Old Brewhouse (in Quay Road) is also a former brewery and there are remains of Avon Brewery in Stanpit.

Christchurch's military tradition continued with cavalry barracks established in Barrack Road in 1795. The Crimean War and Boer War would see men stationed here ready to go off to fight. During WW1 the wounded arrived at Christchurch Station and were taken to the hospital in Fairmile Road.

The Victorians made many changes around Christchurch, their greatest contribution probably being the railway, which enabled people to visit in large numbers and led in time to Wick Ferry Holiday Camp (later Pontins). Curiously, the railway came to Christchurch in three stages: first with a station at Christchurch Road in the New Forest (later Holmsley), 7 miles away, then a station east of Bargates, reached via the light railway (maximum speed 25 mph) from Ringwood, and finally today's station, west of Bargates and just half a mile from the town centre.

Christchurch has a history of boat building. A vessel, *The Trout*, was brought down the Avon from Salisbury, fitted out at Christchurch, then used off Kent's coast in the Hundred Years War. Just off Convent Walk is Elkins Boatyard, which built 220 vessels of all descriptions for the Admiralty during WW2, including over 100 landing craft which participated in all major landing operations, culminating in D-Day. Ian Elkins was the second generation of his family to own the boatyard.

'My father (Ernest Elkins) founded the boatyard around 1927 and was responsible for building the Headland boats, which still operate as ferries on the Stour today. The family moved out of the boatyard during the war because of the bombing risk and was evacuated to Hereford, but the war proved a significant time for the yard. Three boats were being delivered to the Admiralty at a time. A single boat might have been tempting fate, in case of breakdown. Getting in and out of Christchurch Harbour can be difficult for the uninitiated. The Admiralty insisted on collecting the boats on one occasion, but ended up with one damaged and two run aground, so that order was quickly rescinded! The 72-ft patrol boats, used for guarding harbour entrances, were the largest ever launched on the Avon and Stour. They were fantastic boats. We also went on to build powerboats. I had a long association with the boatyard, taking over the business in 1960, building it up and then selling it around 1975/76.'

Bournemouth Boating's Headland boats berthed at Tuckton.

When Ian's father retired, the boatyard was split in two, with one half going to Ian's younger brother Geoff. This half continues the name of Elkins Boatyard today with moorings and mobile homes. A WW2 pillbox on Convent Meadows is a poignant reminder of Elkins' vital work during wartime.

Christchurch played an important part in WW2 also with development of the prototype Bailey Bridge at the Experimental Bridging Establishment on Barrack Road. It was an invention that none other than 'Monty' claimed was instrumental in shortening the war. The town also acted as an 'anti-tank island', with concrete tank 'traps' and pillboxes. Barrack Road was nicknamed 'Pump Alley' before WW2 as it bristled with petrol pumps. There are still two petrol stations in the road today.

Christchurch has a notable aviation history. 'Airspeed' (1939) made a vital contribution in winning WW2 (and after), building Horsa gliders (used on D-Day), Oxford trainers, Vampires, Sea Vixens, Falcons, Mosquito fighter bombers and Ambassadors, becoming part of the De Havilland group, before closing in 1962. Christchurch Airfield (Somerford), where this industry was based and which started as a flying club in 1926, was RAF Christchurch in WW2; it closed in 1964 and is now an industrial estate and housing. Hurn Airport (now Bournemouth) is a survivor from WW2. Cobham plc (founded by Sir Alan Cobham) has had aerial services based at Hurn since the 1970s. Known originally as Flight Refuelling Ltd, it pioneered methods of inflight-refuelling, famously used when a Vulcan bomber attacked an Argentine-held airfield at Port Stanley during the Falklands War (1982).

From early in WW2 to 1980 a Signals Research and Development Establishment (SRDE) was based at Christchurch. During the war the station helped develop radar cover for the south coast, with aircraft flying from Christchurch Airfield helping to test the equipment. Later, at Friars Cliff, two giant weatherproof RADOMEs were constructed to house satellite-tracking equipment. The first British military communications satellite station here received and transmitted signals from/to the first launched British military satellite, as well as tracking foreign satellites, using an aerial dish 12 m in diameter. Much of the early research on night vision was carried out here, as well as research into optical fibres for communications purposes, which benefitted worldwide phone systems. SRDE moved to Malvern, Worcestershire, in 1980 where it joined with the Royal Radar Establishment.

One strange thing about Christchurch is that it has changed counties. Up until 1974 it was part of Hampshire, after which it came under Dorset. Moreover, for a small town, the town has had its share of royal visitors over the centuries.

- King John visited ten times during his 17-year reign, more times than any other monarch. He stayed in Constable's House near Town Bridge and held two courts at the castle. John's fondness for Christchurch was probably due to its proximity to the New Forest hunting grounds.

- Edward I is likely to have visited. He was Lord of the Manor and in 1303 required the Priory to provide a ship for Scottish invasion.
- Edward II, Edward III, Henry VII and Henry VIII are reputed to have stayed at the castle.
- Edward VI is believed to have visited in 1552, when it is said he sat under an oak tree in Verwood and cured people's illnesses, including scrofula, known as 'the King's Evil' (it was believed a touch from the king could heal this skin disease). He also held a privy council, probably at Constable's House.
- George III patronised the town in the 1790s.
- Prince Louis Philippe I, the future French king, took refuge at Priory House during the Napoleonic Wars.
- Princess Victoria is reputed to have visited the George Inn before becoming queen.
- Edward VII stayed at Highcliffe Castle on several occasions as Prince of Wales and monarch. In 1880 he spent time on the beach, swimming to the royal yacht, moored offshore.
- Also in 1880, the future king George V stayed at Highcliffe Castle, aged 15.
- The King and Queen of Norway visited the Priory in 1887.
- The Duke of Connaught (Prince Arthur, third son of Queen Victoria) and Duchess stayed at Highcliffe Castle in late October 1892 and drove into Christchurch.
- The young Spanish King Alfonso XIII visited Highcliffe Castle in 1906, planting a tree (Spanish chestnut) which curiously died shortly before Alfonso abdicated in favour of his son Juan in January 1941 (he had fled the country nearly a decade earlier, but retained his claim to the throne).

HM Kaiser Wilhelm II at a tree-planting ceremony at Highcliffe Castle, 1907. (© Hampshire County Council. Provided by Hampshire Cultural Trust.

- Kaiser Wilhelm II, the German emperor, spent 3 weeks at Highcliffe Castle in 1907. He visited the Priory, admiring the tone of the organ and signing the visitors' book. Popular at this time, it was only 7 years later that he became the most reviled person in England at the start of WW1.
- The Duke of Edinburgh paid the Kings Arms a visit in 1949.
- Queen Elizabeth II and Prince Philip visited the town in 1966, including the Priory. They drove through Highcliffe, where Lymington Road was lined end-to-end with spectators.

Mike Andrews is Christchurch through and through. Born in Tuckton, his grandfather was a Mudeford fisherman, great-grandfather a water bailiff on the Royalty Fishery and great-great-grandfather the last official town crier (there is still a ceremonial crier).

'Christchurch History Society began in 1989 and I was almost in from the beginning. It was formed to sort and catalogue Herbert Druitt's archive, which is still ongoing, but the society now also arranges walks and talks, as well as publishing books and undertaking research for people.

What I love about the town is how important it has been in the past and all the connections you find with people and places, far more than you'd expect from a town of this size. It punches above its weight. The Industrial Revolution largely passed us by, but the town did have the silk stocking and cloth industry (1600–1700s) and then we were a UK centre for fusee manufacturing. Brewing was also important, with, I believe, beer exported to the Navy at Portsmouth and over 30 pubs in the town. I would be fascinated to travel back to either the Priory site or Hengistbury Head about 3,500 years ago to see the Bronze Age people migrating through to Salisbury and Stonehenge from the southern Mediterranean and then travel forward (time-lapse) in 100-year bites to see how this area changed.

For me, Christchurch is right up there and holds its own with anywhere. It has so many layers of history and we are discovering more. Herbert Druitt was a vociferous campaigner for Christchurch and around the same time there was George Brownen, a local historian. More recently we've had Allen "Chalky" White, who wrote several books. The Society aims to keep their archive in the town as well as continuing their work by finding more. The fact that there is more history to be discovered was illustrated recently when I found that WW1 poet Siegfried Sassoon was married to a local girl in Christchurch Priory in 1933 and amongst the guests was T.E. Lawrence (of Arabia).'

The Rivers and Town Quay

River Avon

The Avon flows from Salisbury to Christchurch, and the 34-mile (55-km) Avon Valley Path broadly follows the river's course between the two towns. There are plenty of places where the river can be accessed (see Walk 5). Together with its tributaries, it makes up one of the UK's largest chalk river systems, with river, bank and meadows managed, as they provide homes for animals and plants not found elsewhere (the chalk soils filter and purify the water, making this a great place for wildlife). The meadows are important for breeding waders such as lapwing and redshank, whilst its banks host the elusive water vole. Stay awhile as it's possible you could see an otter. Atlantic salmon return from the sea to the river they were born in. They rest in pools before laying eggs in clean gravel and fast waters. In summer you might see white and yellow flowers floating on the water; these are water crowfoot (water buttercup).

The Avon is a mysterious river which reputedly freezes from the bottom up.

As the river heads towards the Quay, the Mill Stream splits off. Pleasant Convent Walk follows a narrow path from Town Bridge, between these two waterways, to Place Mill and the Quay.

The Royalty Fishery on the Avon dates back to AD 939 and once had a poaching case heard personally by Oliver Cromwell (in 1657). It has been owned by Bournemouth and West Hampshire Water (now Bournemouth Water) since 1929. The Fishery is famed for spring salmon that once averaged 20–30 lb. The largest fish caught with rod and line was claimed by Mr G.M. Howard in 1952 and weighed 49 lb. As recently as 2013 a 31-lb fish was caught at the Railway Pool, just north of the bridge.

The Fishery attracts anglers from all over the world, including the well known, such as 1920–30s racing driver and land speed record-holder Captain George Eyston, rugby union world cup winner Richard Hill, champion jockey Joe Mercer, celebrity chef Marco Pierre White, and screen stars such as Norman Wisdom, Bernard Cribbins, Paul Whitehouse and Chris Tarrant. Royalty Fishery House, overlooking the Avon, used to be the home of the Fishery's keeper but now houses a small museum. Tony Timms is a Royalty Fishery historian and the museum curator and has traced head-keepers back to 1754.

'I've fished here since I was six and love this stretch of river. The Fishery was enormous back in the 1800s and, although smaller now, its place at the heart of Christchurch is secure. The golden salmon on top of the Priory's west tower recalls the days when the prior received a gift of the first salmon of the season.

Royalty Fishery House was built for keeper Frederick Tizzard in the 1880s. He used to take a horse and cart to Hinton Admiral Station to pick up the landed gentry who came for the fishing. Salmon were laid out in the Rod Room after a catch and there would have been three or four rods on the back wall, hence the name. Some keepers were real characters. Montague William Hayter, for example, played first-class cricket for Hampshire in 1904.

Priory weathervane.

Master fisherman Tony Timms on the River Avon Royalty Fishery.

Putting the museum together has been a labour of love, with many exhibits donated, and everyone agrees it is in its rightful place in the Rod Room. I set myself a mission to bring back the two Howard salmon (two 41¾-lb salmon caught by G.M. Howard in 1951). We had casts made from the originals, still in the possession of the Howard family. These hang alongside the record 49-lb salmon in the museum. The last salmon I kept for the table was in 1987. Since then I have released all fish back to the river. This is a "catch and release" fishery today as salmon need all the help they can get. It is possible to stand on the Great Weir, watching salmon jumping and heading up the hatches – amazing sight!'

Inside the Rod Room, a display of record-breaking salmon catches.

River Stour

The River Stour is just over 60 miles (97 km) long, running from its source at Stourhead, Wiltshire, through Dorset to Christchurch, where it is joined by the Avon near Town Quay, both rivers then draining into Christchurch Harbour. The Stour Valley Way is a long-distance footpath from Stourton to Hengistbury Head.

You can walk the short distance from Town Quay to the Captain's Club

The River Stour at Tuckton.

Wick Ferry (the smaller white boat) has been plying its trade since medieval times.

Hotel alongside the Stour, then take the ferry across to Wick (actually part of Bournemouth), walking along the far bank, with splendid views across the river to the Priory. Wick Ferry dates back to at least Norman times and maybe even to the Saxon foundation of Christchurch.

The Captain's Club Hotel occupies the site of former Wick Ferry Holiday Camp, which closed in the 1960s, reopening as Pontins in 1962, before closing forever in 1995. At its height there were 224 chalets on site and 20,000 visitors a year enjoying the holiday camp. A popular regatta has been held on the Quay since 1909, previously centred on Mudeford. Today's finish line is on the Stour at the Rowing Club, just east of the Captain's Club.

Tuckton Bridge was originally a toll bridge.

Tuckton Bridge spanning the river marks one of the boundaries between Christchurch and Bournemouth. A timber bridge was built in 1883, but this was replaced in 1905 with today's concrete structure, which is 110 m long and was designed to take the weight of tramcars. The bridge dictates the limit of navigability for sailing boats. Motor boats can moor further up river and it is possible to continue further inland in small oar or motor-driven craft.

Town Quay

It is hard to believe, looking at Town Quay today, with families having fun, that this was once an industrial quay, where goods were loaded and unloaded. Goods coming in included coal, tea, vinegar, tallow, butter and soap. One of the exports was beer, as there were six breweries in the town at one time. The last commercial vessel docking here was *Gerald*, a 60-ton Thames Barge which came to collect 100-tons of gravel for Newport on the Isle of Wight in 1938; it is a mystery what the IOW wanted with all that gravel, but it's possible it was extracted at Mudeford, as a Thames Barge was pictured at Mudeford Quay *c.* 1938. A coal store once occupied most of the area of today's car park, at the eastern end of the Quay, with the coal barge *Charlotte* making its last visit in 1906. The stone quay was constructed soon after the departure of the last regular trading craft around 1900, which was when the area was reclaimed as a public amenity and the Quay most likely improved.

Town Quay, still busy today, though now for recreation.

The water has frozen here in the past, for example in 1841 and 1855, when the ferry was put out of action, which occurred again nearly a century later in February 1954. The water was frozen once more in the notorious winter of 1962/63, when people were pictured walking, skating and even cycling across the ice. Sadly there was also tragedy when one youngster ventured on to the ice to rescue his dog and lost his life.

On the Quay can be found Place Mill and Quay Cottage (behind the café), whose stone wall in the garden probably belonged to the monastic brew-house or a stable block. The wall was built up in 1986 and became part of a new single-storey building housing an unusual tricycle museum, which sadly closed about a decade later. The two rivers Avon and Stour have their confluence just below Town Quay.

The Quomps and Mayors Mead

The Quomps is the name given to the large grassed area adjacent to the Town Quay and River Stour bordered by Wick Lane, Whitehall, Queens Avenue and Quay Road. It is a popular recreational area, used for many events, including the 'Stompin' on the Quomps' music festival. The area was gifted to the town in 1911 by James Harris, 5th Earl of Malmesbury, and occupies what was an ancient common of around 2 ha which was freely available for grazing, until the land became progressively liable to flooding. 'Quomps' is apparently a Hampshire corruption of two words, quagmire and swamps, and the area used to be marshy but has been reclaimed. Even today, it can be prone to flooding.

The Quomps in flood.

At the rear of the Quomps is the imposing old pumping station (now offices), a necessity in the past prior to construction of modern flood defences. Most of the coal cargoes to the Quay were to service the steam pump engines. The Auxiliary Fire Service once had its headquarters here and in monastic times the canons their fish pond.

The bandstand was constructed in 1938 and financed by a mystery donation of £300, a gift to celebrate the coronation of King George VI and Queen Elizabeth (the mother of Queen Elizabeth II). The cast-iron framework came from the Lion Foundry, Kirkintilloch, near Glasgow. It is now known the benefactor was David Llewellyn, chairman of the town band and general manager of West Hants Water Company.

Mayors Mead at the western end of the Quomps (where the car park is by the splash park and playground) was so named because of a medieval tax whereby the first cut of hay from the meadow had to be sent to the mayor to offset his expenses (the first recorded mayor of Christchurch took office in 1297). When the Miniature Railway was sited here in 1949, the council took 25% of the profits in lieu of rent, so the obligation of Mayors Mead continued. The railway was a popular attraction into the 1980s, but all that remains today is a concrete post close to the playground, which stood by the miniature Christchurch Station.

In February 2015 pupils from Priory School helped plant a tree near the entrance of Mayors Mead car park to commemorate the 70th anniversary of the liberation of Auschwitz. A memorial stone with a black granite plaque was also unveiled. Among those present was the grandson of a couple who died in the camp in 1942.

A bird's eye view of the Quomps, Mayors Mead and sweep of the River Stour from the Priory tower.

Harbour and Seafront

Christchurch Harbour

Christchurch Harbour formed about 7,000 years ago when sea levels rose after the end of the last Ice Age (the Pleistocene epoch). Christchurch (Town) Quay lies in the harbour's upper reaches on the Stour, which flows into the harbour, along with the Avon. The two rivers jointly flow through a narrow channel called 'Steepbank' to the wider harbour, before finally discharging into the sea just beyond Mudeford Quay, a journey of just over 2 miles from Town Quay.

The meeting of the two rivers, viewed from the Priory tower.

The harbour entrance ('The Run') has Mudeford Quay on one side and Hengistbury Head (Mudeford Sandbank) on the other. The water-flow through here can be up to 8 knots and the shallow channel makes it difficult for boats

The tricky harbour entrance.

with a draught of more than 1 m. Shallow-draught boats can enter and cruise upstream for 2 miles, using either the Avon or the Stour. The channel has been marked since at least 1884 and today the red and green buoys are positioned by local fishermen, when necessary. The harbour itself is generally shallow, with a double high water on each tide. Sandbanks are visible at low water, often acting as temporary homes to various species of bird.

Stanpit Marsh adjoins the harbour on its northern side and can be accessed via a pubic footpath from either Two Riversmeet Leisure Centre or Stanpit Recreation Ground. The marsh was formed by deposition from the rivers as they meet the salt water within the harbour. It is extremely low-lying, with its highest point (Crouch Hill) just 5 m above sea level. Blackberry Point, to the east of the marsh, becomes an island at high water.

The harbour is home to a variety of wildlife, with over 320 bird species recorded, and otters and seals have been seen here. There is an abundance of insect life and rare plant species, with habitats of saltmarsh, wet meadow, grassland, heath, sand dune, woodland and scrub.

Mudeford Quay

Mudeford Quay provides spectacular views out to sea and the Isle of Wight and back towards Christchurch and the Priory. Quay Head tends to be the focus for visitors, with its historic buildings, including Haven Cottages (*c.* 1695) and Haven House Inn (*c.* 1840s), a popular pub. At one end of the cottages (also known as Dutch Cottages) is the Old Customs House, now a holiday let. The Dutch reference recalls the fact that cottages were occupied by Dutch dredging experts in the 17th century, employed to improve navigation of the harbour.

At the southern end of Haven House is the original Haven Inn (first recorded in 1699 in a House of Commons Journal) from where smugglers took potshots at a customs cutter during the Battle of Mudeford (1784). Part

The historic buildings on Quay Head lend charm to this popular spot.

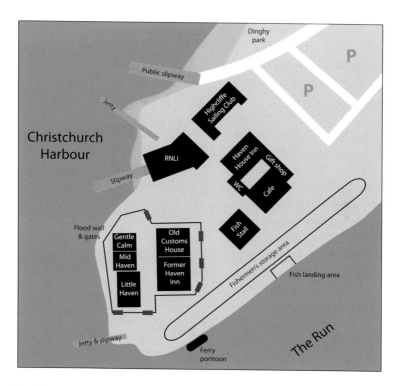

Christchurch Harbour

of this building is now a holiday let (the Water Burrow). The Revenue men had a Preventive Station here from 1823 as they fought running battles with smugglers. It was now the turn of the customs officers to be garrisoned in the Haven and row of cottages built alongside. Smugglers used the group of buildings at the end of the Quay, with spirits imported illicitly, whilst beer ironically was exported lawfully from what was also a working quay. One can only assume that the smugglers lived off their wits with Revenue men breathing down their necks, at least until 1860, when the customs officers moved to cottages in Stanpit.

Mudeford Quay c. 1900. (© Hampshire County Council. Provided by Hampshire Cultural Trust.)

There are a total of seven cottages at Quay Head (Haven Cottages), some owner occupied, others holiday lets, plus today's pub, a café and gift shop. The RNLI and Highcliffe Sailing Club have premises here and the Quay is a popular windsurfing and sailing centre and venue for dinghy championships. Speed boat cruises and mackerel fishing trips are also available.

The fishermen's working area.

Traditional commercial fishing takes place from Quay Head, evidenced by fishing boats and lobster pots. The Fish Stall sells some of the local catch.

On Rogation Sunday (the Sunday before Ascension Day), the local vicar takes to the water in a rowing boat to bless the sea (and encourage a good salmon harvest) in a short religious ceremony.

Blessing the waters at Mudeford, seen from the Quay, c. 1970. (© Hampshire County Council. Provided by Hampshire Cultural Trust.)

Pete Dadds has fished with rod and line since he was 12, when he went out with his elder brother and caught a Dover sole with his first cast. At 18 he had his own fishing boat and is regularly seen at Mudeford Quay, from where he operates.

'It's a hard occupation being a sea fisherman; 14 hours a day, 7 days a week, 3 am starts in summer, but I love it. It's the only life I've known and I couldn't imagine myself doing anything else. I fish within about 3–4 miles, from Bournemouth Pier (west) to Milford (east). I don't need any navigational aid to know where I am, as I know these waters so well. I never aim to put out in bad weather, but sometimes wind can get up and you go from flat calm to storm force in 10 minutes.

There was one occasion when we were crab fishing and it was going so well we continued a bit longer until we'd caught 3 tons, which is our capacity. Heading home, the wind was so fierce you couldn't hear yourself think. 93 knots was recorded at St Catherine's Point (Isle of Wight). Our propeller wash was thrown back over the boat and it took three of us to pull up the mizzen mast, something one person can normally do comfortably. We'd had such a bumper catch, it was adrenaline pulling us through.

Fisherman Pete Dadds, a regular sight on the quayside.

I export some of my catch but also supply local cafés, like the Noisy Lobster (Avon Beach) who take crab, lobster, Dover sole, plaice and turbot. I also deal with a local supplier who sells to local restaurants. He probably takes 95% of my catch. Sometimes I'll be introduced to someone at the Noisy Lobster who's just had one of my fish, and it's always good to get feedback. There is a real community amongst the fishermen and we all help one another. When I first started fishing out of Mudeford over 20 years ago, we had two-dozen boats, but now we're down to just five. Fish quotas haven't helped and youngsters don't seem to want to take it up these days; however, having said that, my little girl loves the boat, so maybe she's the next generation!'

Pete is also a volunteer helmsman on the Mudeford lifeboat. The fishermen were instrumental in establishing a lifeboat station at Mudeford in 1963, but Pete is now the only fisherman amongst 16 crew members. In November 2014, in his fishing boat, he went to the aid of a lone sailor who had been thrown overboard. He received a meritorious award from the Borough Council in April 2015.

'I like to think that I bring my local knowledge to bear, which helps my fellow crew members. I also train the others in seamanship and boat handling. We have 16 crew members, but it's the first four to respond who go out on any call-out. The crew here trains hard. They're all willing to learn and we have such a mix of occupations (everything from ambulance driver to air-traffic control instructor) that they all bring their own expertise. By the end of the year we will probably have had 50 "shouts" (call-outs) and we also have exercises each month.

The RNLI operates from a modern (2003) boat house, a 'Discover' station that welcomes visitors.

We are the seventh busiest station on the south coast and whilst the majority of incidents will result in "tow-ins", we do get medical emergencies and situations involving children, which "up the ante". We try to deal with each incident as quickly and safely as possible, but each case has to be treated on its merits. The Mudeford station currently has an inshore lifeboat, an "Atlantic 85" (8.5 m in length) rigid inflatable, which is good for force 7 or 8. We aim to put the crew and boat through its paces, so when we have a real emergency everyone has total confidence.'

The large grassed area beyond the RNLI and dinghy area is ideal for picnics and recreation, although the most popular activity at the Quay for families seems to be 'crabbing', favoured spots being along the promenade adjacent to the car park and the end of the Quay overlooking the harbour. Crab lines can be purchased in the shop at Haven Café and bait from the Fish Stall.

It is possible to take a passenger and cycle ferry from the Quay to Mudeford Sandbank to explore Hengistbury Head SSSI. The ferry runs approximately every 12 minutes in season. Harbour cruises of 1¼ hours' duration operate year-round for groups of between 6 and 60, subject to tidal conditions.

The Derhams have been a Christchurch family since about 1750, including churchwardens at the Priory. Paul Derham has owned the Mudeford Ferry Company since 2004:

'I was 27 years with P&O Cruises before I bought this business, so my life has always been on the water. There were rowing ferries originally, one of which is preserved in the Red House Museum, then motor ferries (two when I bought the business but now we have five). The ferry from Mudeford Quay to Mudeford Sandbank is our bread and butter, although we also do harbour/river cruises and fast boat trips. In the winter we work weekends and school holidays, then daily from end of March to end of October, when our motto is "every day in British summertime", and the 6-week summer holiday sees the ferry operating between 9 am and 10 pm. We have a flagpole on Mudeford Quay (when the flag is flying we are running).

We have a nucleus of four skippers, plus college-age students in the summer act as crew. Every crossing is different, with other boats to navigate around and

'Derham's Houseboat Teas and Luncheon' anchored in the harbour off the spit. These boats were popular between the wars. (© Hampshire County Council. Provided by Hampshire Cultural Trust.)

constantly changing weather, tides and wildlife. I have seen seals and otters and we also do dolphin trips if we've seen them on the two previous days. The bigger ships have a tannoy so we can provide commentary on harbour trips and during Dorset Architectural Heritage Week. We also do "Red-Arrows Trips" during Bournemouth Air Show. Quite a few celebrities have used our boats including Chris Evans, Billie Piper, Howard Donald, Pauline Quirke, Harry Redknapp, Christine Hamilton and Charlie Dimmock.'

Gundimore Promenade and Avon Beach

A pleasant walk can be undertaken from the Quay along Gundimore Promenade to Avon Beach. You pass Sandhills Holiday Park, taking its name from 'Sandhills', the late-18th-century white mansion in the centre of the complex once owned by George Rose, MP (1744–1818), who built the Kings Arms. Rose was a close friend of Nelson and was invited on *HMS Victory*

before the ship sailed for Trafalgar. Previously Rose had been involved in sending the 'First Fleet' to the new penal colony of New South Wales, Australia, in 1787.

Sandhills, part of the holiday scene at Avon Beach.

Avon Beach has its own café and shop, beach huts, canoe and deck-chair hire. The Avon Beach Company was run by four generations of the Derham family from 1934, before being sold in 2013. As well as the café and shop, the business owns and looks after a quarter mile of beach and 125 beach huts. There is a handy beachside car park at the end of Mudeford Lane, which had the charming name of 'The Peep', derived from the restricted view from the road looking down towards the beach.

Friars Cliff and Steamer Point

Further along is Friars Cliff, with its colourful beach huts and own café called the Beach Hut, which opens specially on Christmas morning to raise money for Macmillan Cancer Support. A New Year's Day swim also takes place here to benefit the charity, with members of Christchurch Life Saving Club represented. A lifeguard and first-aid service operates here in summer and the area is designated for water sports. There is also a former coastguard training school building and a cliff-top monument marking the site of a radar development station.

Continuing on from Friars Cliff is Steamer Point and the grounds of Highcliffe Castle, which can be accessed via a zig-zag path up the cliff. This is a designated windsurfing area and a round of the annual UK national championships is held here. Steamer Point Nature Reserve is a short walk from the beach. A sign at Friars Cliff Beach shows the location of the reserve, next to Seaway Avenue car park.

From Friars Cliff there are magnificent views of the Isle of Wight and Christchurch Bay.

Steamer Point takes its name from the steamer *SS Arrow* that Highcliffe Castle's owner, Lord Stuart de Rothesay, pulled up the beach to a gap in the cliff in 1830 and used as a site office, then summer house. Now long since gone, the steamer reveals its boiler sometimes at low tide.

Orienteering markers are scattered throughout the nature reserve, beach and Highcliffe Castle, part of the Activate Coast and Countryside project, which gives people the chance to try out a range of different sporting activities. Orienteering packs are available to buy from the Castle gift shop, or you can book a 3-hour instructor-led session.

In May 2015 Avon Beach, Friars Cliff Beach and Highcliffe Beach all won Seaside Awards (judged and presented by Keep Britain Tidy) for achieving the highest standards of beach management and for meeting water quality guidelines.

Nature Areas and Gardens

There are 23 named nature areas in the Borough of Christchurch, which the council maintains. However, there is much more green space than this, with other wildlife areas. For example, the Commons comprise 142 ha of land and cover three areas – Town Common (the slopes and base of St Catherine's Hill), Cowards Marsh (off Marsh Lane) and Ogber (north of Christchurch on the Avon floodplain). Of 5,171 ha comprising the borough, 576 ha are natural or semi-natural (over 11%).

Peter Holloway, born at Tuckton, is the Senior Countryside Officer. His first job was as a summer warden at Stanpit Marsh and he has continued working in this field.

'I love Christchurch's diversity in flora and fauna. We have all UK reptiles represented on our heathlands, also nearly a quarter of plant and bird species. I believe our mission is to protect the local distinctiveness that we're blessed with, namely wetlands, flower meadows, heaths, cliff-top woods and coastline. You would have to go some distance to find something comparable.

I like the variety my job entails, working on strategy and management plans to ensure habitats are properly cared for, gathering evidence to support the Council's policy of protection, whilst ensuring people can access and enjoy open spaces. We have an army of willing volunteers, enabling us to do more than would otherwise be possible and they come from every walk of life – botanists, photographers, historians – bringing different skills to nature conservation. Our first volunteer from over 30 years ago is still attending and he's over 80 now!

We aim to make people feel welcome and engaged, hopefully providing expert guidance needed to help protect wildlife for years to come. Some people visited as children and return with their own children, for whom there are many educational opportunities, with nature groups, for example. The information centre at Steamer Point is very popular and was the first public building in Dorset to have solar panels, something we hope to roll out. The newer Stanpit Marsh Information Centre, built with the help of funds

Eco-friendly Stanpit Marsh Visitor Centre.

from Friends of Stanpit Marsh, is an example of working with the community. It won a Local Authority Building Control award for best sustainable development. The continued involvement of people in looking after local open spaces is vital to a sustainable service and healthy environment for all.'

Stanpit and Purewell

Stanpit Marsh

Just below the confluence of the rivers Avon and Stour on Christchurch Harbour's north side lies Stanpit Marsh, 65 ha of creeks and salt pans, reed beds, saltwater and freshwater marsh. Together with connected Grimbury Marsh, it is one of the largest areas of salt marsh in the county, an SSSI and nature reserve. It has over 300 species of plants, including 14 that are nationally rare.

In spring the Marsh is covered in red sheep's sorrel, with flowering rush and marsh-mallow in places.

Stanpit Marsh is home to many birds and an important stopover for migratory birds such as whimbrels, godwits and shell duck. Little egret and heron breed on Hengistbury Head and are often seen feeding on the marsh. Red kite have also been spotted.

A little egret stalks the Marsh.

The herd of New Forest ponies (numbering 15–28) belong to a grazier. Most have lived here all their life, doing an important job of keeping scrub at bay.

The marsh has been a human refuge since the Middle Stone Age, through 18th-century smugglers hauling contraband up creeks, to today's nature lovers. A natterjack toad breeding programme has operated since 2001. There is a prototype Bailey Bridge. Ashtree Meadow is just east of Two Riversmeet Leisure Centre, just south of Purewell to the very north of Stanpit Marsh, and Monkswell Green is a piece of fen/wetland adjacent to Ashtree Meadow.

Stanpit also encompasses a reed bed close to the Ship in Distress, and Tutton's Well, the last remaining natural mineral spring within a public open space in East Dorset ('wella' being Anglo-Saxon for 'spring'). It was known for its purity and medicinal properties as long ago as the Middle Ages, when its water was conveyed around the country as a cure, known as 'Christchurch Elixir'. The well, once Stanpit's only source of fresh water, can be found a few metres south of Stanpit Recreation car park, in the direction of Mudeford (see Walk 2).

Purewell Meadows

The 14-ha reserve of the River Avon floodplain wet meadow is divided into public open space, and SSSI with no public access. Kestrel, marbled white butterfly, devil's bit scabious, marsh marigold, heath spotted orchid, mother shipton moth and palmate newts are present. The open area is in between the Christchurch by-pass and Purewell Cross Road. On-road parking is available in Scott's Hill Lane and Burton Road.

Highcliffe

Steamer Point

A rare cliff-top woodland nature reserve covering 10 ha, Steamer Point lies between Highcliffe Castle and Friars Cliff and includes an information centre where the Countryside Service is based. During WW2, Steamer Point was the site of a military radar research station and sentry boxes survive from this time. Nuthatch, woodpecker and white admiral butterfly are among today's residents. Rothesay Woods is part of the reserve.

Steamer Point nature reserve, originally intended as a formal and functional woodland, with salt-tolerant tree species such as Holm Oak planted to help stabilise the cliff.

Chewton Bunny and Chewton Gateway

Chewton Bunny is a pleasant woodland walk alongside Walkford Brook to the sea.

'Bunny' is a local name for valley and Chewton's version is a short distance from central Highcliffe. It is an area of ancient woodland, rich in wildlife. Centrally placed Mill House, a former grain mill on Walkford Brook, is now a private home, looking down on a smugglers' route, and north of this is the first-ever reinforced concrete bridge, which goes over the freshwater stream. The site is noted for opposite-leaved golden saxifrage, wood anemone, nuthatch, woodpecker and dog's mercury.

'Chewton Gateway' is an area of derelict woodland southwest of Chewton Common; it is accessed by a footpath at the rear of Highcliffe Medical Centre.

Nea Meadows, Hazelmere Copse, Lakewood and Cliffs SSSI

Close to Highcliffe are 5 ha comprising Nea Meadows, a mixture of woodland, wetland, meadow and recreational park, part of the former estate of Nea House, a large 18th-century property demolished in 1940. Some landscaping, woodland and parts of the original fishpond survive from that era. Recreation includes coarse fishing on the main lake and public bowling at Highcliffe Bowling Club. Over 250 species of wildflower have been recorded, including broad-leaved helleborine orchids, as well as birds such as kingfisher and little egret, emperor dragonfly and purple hairstreak butterfly.

Hazelmere Copse is a further plot in Highcliffe (off Hazelmere Avenue, near Highcliffe St Mark Primary School), whilst Lakewood is a pond situated on a roundabout (at the junction of Braemar Drive and Lakewood Road). Cliffs SSSI extends from Highcliffe to Milford.

The main lake at Nea Meadows was constructed in 1987/88 with the primary purpose of flood defence. Christchurch Angling Club members enjoy fishing here.

Mudeford

Mude Valley

Mudeford and Peregrine Woods make up the 17.5-ha Mude Valley Nature Reserve, which follows the River Mude from Somerford (north) to Mudeford

Mudeford Wood offers a a diversity of habitats and is a Site of Nature Conservation and Interest.

(south). Habitats include woodland, grassland, river and wetlands. Human use is thought to date to when monks of Somerford Grange kept a pond for farming carp. Today's angling pond is leased to the Mudeford Wood Angling Club and contains a selection of coarse fish, including perch, bream and common carp. Dragonflies, damselflies, butterflies, song thrush and bullfinch (amongst 47 bird varieties) can be seen, plus stone loach, bullhead, lamprey, eel and trout in the river.

North of Christchurch

St Catherine's Hill

St Catherine's Hill, 35 ha of heathland and coniferous forest and Christchurch's highest area (50 m above sea level), lies to the north of the town. Spectacular views can be gained, explaining why the hill was used as a lookout and beacon possibly since prehistoric times and certainly at the time of the Armada. The hill has been used by the military, including in both World Wars for trench warfare and grenade-throwing practice. The heathland is precious, yet threatened by invasive species that need controlling. With Dartford warbler, sand lizard, smooth snake, adder, nightjar, silver-studded blue and scarce chaser butterflies, and white-legged damselfly to protect, there is much to fight for.

The Friends of St Catherine's Hill started in 2008 and run a full programme of events. Chris Gordon is one of its 100-plus members.

'The Friends is committed to ensuring the wellbeing and continued benefit of the hill to the public and wildlife and works with the local council, Amphibian and Reptile Conservation Trust, the water company and West Christchurch Residents' Association to actively manage the hill for this purpose. There is a tree-felling licence in play to restore some land to lowland heath, and we have

St Catherine's Hill, managed in a sensitive way, benefits both people and wildlife.

been active ensuring tree-felling is proportionate with effects monitored. The Friends also run a biennial History Day on the hill, now attended by over 300, as well as seasonal walks, like the "reptile ramble". A new information stone was installed in 2014 at the trig-point (viewpoint), which identifies key points of interest, including the Priory and Isle of Wight, and is a further amenity for hill users. The hill is a special place, close to local amenities and yet a haven of peace, where you can see deer, foxes and more birdlife than you would ever see in the average garden.'

Grove Copse

Grove Copse is adjacent to Hurn Way/Stour Way and close to St Catherine's Hill, so a visit to this mature 1-ha woodland could be combined with a hike up the Hill. Once part of Grove Farm (now a private house next to the site), it was called 'Bluebell Wood', although only patches remain. Rooks, jackdaws, woodpeckers, red admiral butterflies and foxes can be seen here.

Cowards Marsh

Whilst many communities have lost common land, Christchurch tenaciously holds on to what it has. Cowards (Cowherd's) Marsh is an area of common land comprising 28 ha of rich (Avon) river meadow. It is accessed from the unmade part of Marsh Lane, past Marsh House, which is occupied by the herdsman. Christchurch Commoners must be residents of Twynham or Portfield wards and pay council tax in order to graze animals here – from

Lammas to Candlemas (May–February), with a 3-month rest period. The maximum number allowed is twelve cattle (excluding bulls) or six horses, donkeys or mules per head in the household. The marsh is also popular with swans.

Nicky Simpson has been Head Steward of Christchurch Commoners' Association since October 1998. She has lived in Christchurch all her life and her love of the marsh and its livestock goes back to childhood.

'I remember aged nine or ten seeing a young horse on its back with a hind leg caught and twisted in wire fencing. Sam Avery came to the rescue with wire cutters and the story had a happy ending. I love to see horses galloping. They have a herd mentality and will all gallop at least once a day. We have a lot of young stock, under 5 years, so they are quite frisky. We're lucky to have a really natural environment with shelter, water and limited fences, as natural an environment as anywhere in England. Horses can be horses, so when they gallop you see them behaving as social animals, doing what comes naturally.

My role is to oversee the general day-to-day running of the marsh and livestock in conjunction with the second steward. The herdsman looks after things on a day-to-day basis, including a daily check on the animals, and reports any issues or concerns to me. I will then either deal with the issues or report them to the committee for consideration and action.

We've had to adapt as there are fewer commoners grazing animals. By allowing others to graze on the marsh we have kept the whole thing viable. Today we balance the needs of all groups wanting to use the marsh: grazers, bird watchers, shooters, fishermen and ramblers. We have a voluntary committee that meets twice a year. There is an AGM in October and a May meeting to confirm whether the marsh is opening or not. In 2013 the opening was delayed 5 weeks, which was unprecedented, as the marsh had been under water. The commons is run like the New Forest. We feel we are custodians of these traditions and want to carry them on for the good of the marsh.'

A home for the herdsman – Marsh House.

Lisa Kinsella is the current herdsman and therefore occupies Marsh House, a traditional cob building, which had no mains electricity when she moved in and still has no central heating.

'Marsh House has had money spent on it, some raised through a Marsh Fair, as we want to keep a herdsman living on site. There is a modern extension at the back, where we hold meetings for committee and commoners, and there is less risk of flooding as the floor has been "tanked". It is still a cold building though so fleeces are mandatory!

My responsibilities are making sure the stock is where it should be, boundaries are in good order and animals' welfare maintained. If there is an issue with a specific animal, I speak to the owner and either isolate it or ask the owner to take it away. I ensure there are no injuries and animals are in general good health; for example, feet have to be in good condition before they go on the marsh, as it is so wet they can suffer foot abscesses. They also need worming at the gate. The cattle are prone to liver fluke, which is spread by snails laying eggs, which the cattle then ingest when eating, which is the main thing to worm against.

We have probably the optimum number of animals on the marsh now. They live in a herd and learn their place within the pecking order. Many more animals and we'd probably start to see squabbling breaking out! It's good to have a "lead cow". She proves her worth when I need to get animals somewhere, say into the pens. It pays to build a relationship with that animal. My current lead cow likes apples and carrots! They're doing their job (wandering and grazing) and horses and cattle together keep vegetation down, which is good for the health of the marsh. The late Benny the Bull was a character. On one occasion a Hereford escaped from Burton, managed to cross the river and started eyeing up Benny's cows, which didn't impress him one bit. He corralled the "ladies" into a corner, maintaining vigil until the interloper had been repatriated.'

Other Nature Sites

Other nature sites are Bure Woods (Bure Lane), the Officers' Mess Nature Reserve (Dragoon Way off Barrack Road), recalling 200 years of the barracks, Roeshot Copse (Roeshot Hill) and Stocker's Mead (the 'Meridians').

Druitt Gardens and Flowers

The gardens behind Christchurch High Street were originally an Edwardian garden belonging to the Druitts. After 30 years of neglect, removal of non-native plants and replacement by native wildlife-friendly species has started to improve the wildlife and amenity value. Also the thinning of sycamores has allowed more light and warmth into the gardens.

Druitt Gardens, a calm oasis, just off the High Street behind the library.

Christchurch won 'Best Town' in Britain in Bloom in 1996, then concentrated on South and South East in Bloom. Former Open Spaces and Countryside Manager for Christchurch Council, Clive Sinden has lived here since 1989 and has resisted all temptations to move.

'The environment here takes some beating. It's a place that holidaymakers want to visit after all, and we're lucky enough to work here. Christchurch has always

been known for flowers. Whilst the Council no longer coordinates, we encourage voluntary groups, such as residents planting Priory Quay and Friends of Christchurch Station. Part of our role is supporting the community and, in so doing, promoting Christchurch. We ensure the planting looks best in July and August for holidaymakers. We were first in the south to introduce barrier baskets [flower troughs on railings] and also first in the area to have roundabout sponsorship. More recently, introducing wildflower beds has gone down well; they encourage butterflies and insects and people love that. We regard

Putting on a display in Christchurch.

planting as always a work in progress as we strive for best practice.'

Keeping Christchurch floral, tidy and appealing is a full-time but rewarding job, which involves more than simply planting seasonal flower beds. Clive sums it up:

'We are responsible for allotments (five sites), Jumpers Cemetery, beaches, promenade and a number of countryside sites, including SSSIs such as Stanpit Marsh and St Catherine's Hill. In addition the small team manages the borough's trees and all the children's playgrounds, of which there are currently 28. Life is never dull!'

New Zealand Garden in Barrack Road Recreation Ground commemorates links with Christchurch, NZ.

Local Fare

Country Market

Every Monday (9.30–11.30 am) a Country Market is held in Druitt Hall behind the library. Everything on offer is locally home-baked, homemade and home-grown, and refreshments are available.

Fish Stall, Mudeford Quay

Aged 14, Highcliffe-born Russell Laker helped to build the Fish Stall, little realising one day he would be its owner. Later, when he built the extension, he could see the business's potential and was in the right place when it came up for sale in 1999.

'We buy what we can locally, although the fishermen here can't supply all we need. We take fish off the boats though and also from rod-and-line fishermen on the beach (e.g. sea bass). Local cod, Dover sole, plaice, brill, turbot, mackerel, dog fish (huss), skate, flounder, conger eel and red mullet are the most common and we get these in most days. Halibut and lemon sole can't be caught in these waters though and tuna and swordfish have to be flown in. Salmon fillet generally comes from Norway. Crab and lobster are always local and we keep these in aerated tanks.

A selection from the counter.

The stall is open every day except Christmas Day and the summer is crazy, as the quay is a different place. It's really hard work then. We also do a lot of deliveries. We have two vans out every day operating over a 25-mile radius. We provide free delivery, which helps out many elderly customers who can't come to the quay. We bone and skin fish and provide advice on cooking too. This is a very personal service and it's always nice to get feedback from customers. One of the funny things that happens though is we get people turning up asking for fish and chips and, of course, we're a fresh fish stall, not a fish and chip shop, so sadly, we have to disappoint them!'

Russell was featured in the BBC series *Invasion of the Job Snatchers* in 2014 when he acted as mentor to youngsters trying to get into employment.

One of the few places you can buy fish straight off the boat.

Pick-Your-Own

The Cat and Fiddle Farm PYO on Lyndhurst Road grows nearly 20 different fruit and vegetables, some for PYO, some for selling ready picked through its own farm shop, and some for sale at farmers' markets and events such as Christchurch's Food and Wine Festival. The farm shop also sells Dorset honey and free-range eggs. There is a sister PYO at Sopley Farm.

Dorset Smokery

The Smokery in Hurn Court Lane was established on the site of the disused Merritown Farm dairy in 1996. It has its own smokehouse, selling smoked fish, duck, sausages, BBQ ribs, chicken, bacon, cheese, salami, biltong (dried, cured meat), pate, Dorset snails, hampers, chutneys and relishes from its deli (The Kitchen by the Smokery). Cookery workshops are also available.

Smokery and charcuterie products from a certified smokehouse. Dorset Smokery was voted Top Aritsan Pate Producer in 2013 by Lovefood.com.

Farm Shop and Delis

Owls Barn Farm Shop in Derritt Lane, Sopley, was converted from the old wheelwright's workshop on the former Sopley estate in 1995. It sells cuts of meat, homemade sausages and burgers, plus fruit and vegetables from local farms.

Located in Christchurch High Street, Heartizans is a family deli/café, making food in its own kitchen using local produce from Christchurch, Dorset and Hampshire, where available, and stocking foods produced by local artisan operators. Dorset Blue Vinny is sold here. Blue Sky Deli on Lymington Road in Highcliffe promotes home-cooked food and aims to bring as many local food producers as possible to the store. Local produce and homemade goods are its staples.

Local Cafés

Christchurch is blessed with a multitude of cafés, coffee shops and tea houses. Two long-standing businesses in the town centre are the New Forest Perfumery and Kelly's Kitchen.

Previously a perfumery mixing New Forest flower perfumes for sale, the New Forest Perfumery is family-run. Owned by Lindsay Case, a Dorset girl whose dream was to run a tea room, the food is complemented by a team that scores points for friendliness and politeness, one of the reasons why they were voted best tea room/café in Christchurch in the 2013 Best of the Best awards. Lindsay says:

'I fell in love with the New Forest Perfumery the first time I saw it. It was August Bank Holiday 2012, the duck race was taking place on the Mill Stream and I had a cream tea on the busiest day of the year. I could see the potential immediately. We aim to make this the quintessential, traditional, romantic tea room. We try to source as much food as possible

Al fresco dining in the courtyard at the New Forest Perfumery.

locally. Most fruit and veg come from Sopley. Our clotted cream is Dorset and jam is New Forest, so we do pretty well with cream teas. Scones are made in a big round tray and quartered – "That's a scone and a half" is the usual comment! We are introducing more home-cooked food and even breakfasts are healthy – nothing fried!'

Living in what is reputed to be 'the oldest council house in the borough', dating back to Medieval times, has its pros and cons.

'It is a fragile, rickety, noisy, characterful building. There are no straight walls, everything is angled, and upstairs is hilarious, bowing in the middle, with a drop of 1 ft either end. I almost knocked myself out once head-butting overhead beams. We eat out in the courtyard on summer evenings though and feel so fortunate with the castle overlooking us and the bells of the Priory chiming away.'

Kelly's Kitchen has been a fixture in the High Street since 1993. Using local suppliers is fundamental to owner Terry Kelly:

'Almost everything is local and we deal with local independent traders. Our main supplier is only 2 miles away [Gibsons Frozen Foods] and another local supplier provides fresh produce, including dairy, on a daily basis [Harvest Fine Foods]. A bakery in Southbourne provides cakes. Our most distant supplier is a farm near Dorchester. Service is important and we know our local suppliers won't let us down. Our main supplier has been with us since the beginning.'

Kelly's Kitchen has a strong loyal customer base.

The Arts

A History of Art and Artists in the Area

John Cantiloe Joy (1806–67) was a marine artist employed by the Admiralty in Portsmouth. Whilst staying with relatives in Christchurch (Edward Joy at The Eight Bells) he painted *Cricket Match on Stanpit Marsh*, which once belonged to Herbert Druitt but now forms part of the Lord's collection.

Augustus Welby Northmore Pugin (1812–52), architect, designer, artist and critic, lived in Christchurch for a while, designing and carving the Priory's altar table. A leader of the Neo-Gothic movement, Pugin is most famous for collaborating with Charles Barry on the interior of the Houses of Parliament after the 1834 fire.

Benjamin Ferrey (1818–80), best known as an architect, also painted seven watercolours to illustrate his book *The Antiquities of the Priory of Christ-Church, Hampshire* (1841). The paintings are in the Priory's St Michael's Loft Museum.

Louisa Stuart, Lady Waterford (1818–91), one of the Victorian era's most gifted amateur women artists, painted watercolours of figures and Biblical scenes. Three of her pictures are in St Mark's Church, Highcliffe. She inherited Highcliffe Castle from her mother.

Minny Stuart painted a book of watercolours of Highcliffe and Mudeford in the mid-19th century. The Stuarts owned Hoburne House in West Highcliffe (demolished in 1967). Later residents included the three talented Shipman sisters (after WW2), all artistically inclined, who exhibited many beautiful paintings in the house.

Admiral George Vernon Jackson married Jane Oldham Johnson, a watercolourist from Kirkby, Liverpool, in 1842, and together they lived at 'Verno', Roeshot Hill, Christchurch.

Edmund Morison Wimperis (1835–1900), English wood engraver and professional landscape watercolour artist, is buried in Christchurch Cemetery, Jumpers Road.

Cmdr Orford Somerville Cameron RN (1836–1921) was an accomplished artist and collector of ceramics and shells. He was baptised in Christchurch and later lived at Burton Close, which exists today, albeit in altered form.

Arthur George Bell (1849–1916) moved to Southbourne in 1889, illustrating Christchurch in his book *From Harbour to Harbour*.

Gleeson White (1852–98) was born at Caxton House Bookshop (now the Regent Centre). He was an artist, illustrator, author and first editor (1895) of *The Studio* art magazine. He traded at the bookshop as a bookseller himself.

Wilfred Williams Ball (1853–1917) was best known for his English landscapes, a watercolour of Place Mill (1908) providing the jacket illustration for Barbara Softly's book of the same name.

Portrait painter **Frank Brooks** (1854–1937) had a studio in the grounds of Shortwood House, Magdalen Lane, Portfield, the building that was Monty's HQ for a period after Dunkirk. Brooks painted the last portrait of King George V before his death.

Louis Raemaekers (1869–1956) was a Dutch painter and cartoonist noted for his anti-German stance in WW1, which led to the German government putting a price on his head. During the war, Raemaekers visited the Priory, pointedly signing the visitors' book immediately under the Kaiser's signature.

Caroline Lassells, a watercolour artist, lived at Winkton Lodge, later Homefield School, Salisbury Road, Winkton (which was then redeveloped as housing).

The Art Scene Today

Christchurch Arts Guild was set up in 1948 for artists in and around Christchurch. It has regular meetings and activities, meetings being held at All Saints Church Hall, Mudeford. Members' work is exhibited at both Red House Museum and Priory House. **Highcliffe Art Fellowship** dates back to 1962 and is a club for artists in Highcliffe. Monthly meetings are held at the Methodist Hall on Lymington Road. The **Peggy Wood Art Group** has existed since about 1978. Members choose their own subjects to paint and meet at Christchurch Rowing Club.

CADArts (Christchurch and District Arts Council) was established in 1978 to promote local arts and act as a coordinating body for individuals and organisations in all fields of the arts. It organises exhibitions and events around Christchurch and every 3 years hosts a celebration of local creativity ('Living Crafts'). A twice-yearly diary of events is produced, available on the website www.cadarts.co.uk and printed as a free brochure. Over 40 local arts groups are represented by CADArts, from camera clubs to singers, writers to embroiderers, floral societies to spinners and weavers.

Since December 2001 CADArts has leased the **Hayloft Studio and Gallery**, organising a summer festival, with workshops, and Christmas exhibition, when members' work is displayed. For the rest of the year the venue can be

CADArts organises many events throughout the year and is a registered charity. You do not need to be a skilled artist/artisan to be a member, just have an interest in the Arts. (Courtesy of CADArts.)

hired by artists and crafts people. The Hayloft is a former coach house and stable, tucked away down Wick Lane. It exhibits original, locally made arts and crafts (paintings, textiles, wood, pottery, jewellery and photography).

Art exhibitions are also held regularly at **Highcliffe Castle**, in its Stateroom Galleries (Library Gallery and Ante-Library Gallery), in the **Regent Centre** foyer and at the **Kings Arms** (Georgian Room). **Red House Museum** also has changing exhibitions. **Priory House** has paintings displayed but no longer has regular exhibitions. **Highcliffe Art Fellowship** hosts a 3-week free exhibition at the Methodist Church Hall, Lymington Road, from the end of July, the largest in the district with around 400 pictures displayed. **Mudeford Quay Arts Festival** is held annually in late July on the Quay's picnic green and celebrates the best of local art and craft.

Bookends in the High Street has a first-floor gallery with a constantly changing display of prints, ranging from traditional to contemporary, including work by local photographers. **Hatch Gallery** in Church Street specialises in British contemporary art, ceramics, handmade jewellery and driftwood furniture and also hosts regular exhibitions.

Although Christchurch is not overly blessed with outdoor art, don't miss the sculpture by Corfe-Castle-based sculptor **Jonathan Sells**. His was the winning design in a competition commemorating the 900th anniversary of the Priory in 1994, and in describing it he says, 'I wanted to create a feeling of rejoicing and celebration, but with a humorous angle.' It can be found near the lily pond in the garden by Place Mill and graces the second page of this book.

Some Local Artists

Jewellery and silversmithing classes are offered by **Louise Taylor** in Christchurch. A variety of techniques are covered, including soldering, enamelling and stone setting. **Susan Knights**, a member of the Society of Floral Painters, runs workshops and classes in watercolour at Stanpit Village Hall, overlooking the Harbour. **Anna Sims** also offers art classes. She teaches adults and children in all mediums in her 100-year-old cottage in Millhams Street. Husband Alan is a sculptor. Their small cottage garden is open through the National Gardens Scheme. **Julie Fisher** has developed the comical 'Fun Hearts' characters, which have large eyes and distinctive heart-shaped noses. Paintings and greeting cards can be viewed on Julie's website. Another local artist, **Peter Castle**, exhibited at the Regent Centre in January 2015, including a '27 Club' series of portraits dedicated to the many talented musicians and artists who all died spookily at that young age (Brian Jones, Jimi Hendrix, Janis Joplin, Jim Morrison and Amy Winehouse being just five).

In 2006 **Chérie Wheatcroft** began exhibiting at Place Mill and is now resident artist there.

'I exhibit from April to October and enjoy being on site, discussing art with customers. The mill is not the easiest place to exhibit; it can be damp and cold, and we need to watch the tides, but this is outweighed by its character and the people that come from every corner of the globe. It also has the advantage of differing light, with daylight coming through, dark shadows and old crooked walls lit up by artist's spotlights – it all gives a unique ambience and enables me to demonstrate how my pictures change in different light. It is a beautiful place to exhibit, with the millstream, Priory, gardens and rivers in close proximity, plus there is always local wildlife to enjoy.'

Place Mill, from old mill to art exhibition space.

Chérie's hand-painted copy of the original village sign on stainless steel.

One interesting commission was to repaint the historic borough sign at Somerford. According to the plaque there, 'Following a speech by HRH the Duke of York at the Royal Academy in 1920 on the revival of village signs, the *Daily Mail* organised a village signs competition and exhibition, offering a total of £2200 in prizes. Ten awards were made and the design from which this sign was constructed secured fourth prize of £100.' The original sign had completely eroded and was restored by Chérie in 2012; it is now back in its rightful place, radiant and bright, providing a marker for people coming into the borough.

Books and Authors

Christchurch Writers and Regent and Hinton Writers are two local writing groups. The town's history has been written about extensively by the likes of **Michael Hodges**, **Sue Newman**, **John Needham**, **Eric Cockain** and **Bill Hoodless** (see Bibliography). **Allen White** (1919–97) was a well-known local historian who produced about a dozen booklets on Christchurch and its history.

Local author **Michael Stannard** writes both fiction (*John Draper's Treasure – A Tale of Christchurch* and *Hugh of Tyneham*) and non-fiction (*Christchurch Priory* and *The Makers of Christchurch: A Thousand Year Story*). **Ian Kingsley**'s *Sandman* is a psychological thriller set on Mudeford sandbank. **Louise Gillett** was also inspired to write about Mudeford, in her collection of poems entitled *Mudeford Quay and Other Poems*. **Anton Evans**' *Where Does the Sun Set?* tells the story of a Purewell author who grew up with a rare disease, and aims to help other families who have children with disabilities. **Julie Ratcliffe** writes children's novels and explains where she gets her inspiration from:

> 'My first book, *The Thirteenth Box*, is a fast-paced children's novel based around the realism of Christchurch's rich 18th-century smuggling tradition. It was not something I wanted to romanticise. I followed this with *The Face of Sam* ... My emphasis is on the story, which I want to be a good read. The history is secondary, but I want it as accurate as possible, prompting children to take greater interest in their town, looking at Christchurch in more detail and learning about events that shaped it. ... This area has certainly been inspirational as far as smugglers' tales are concerned.'

Past literary figures connected with Christchurch include **Richard Warner** (1763–1857), who attended the school in St Michael's Loft, going on to write works on History, Geography and Literature. Writer and poet laureate **Robert Southey**, who lived in Burton in 1797–99, was visited by his brother-in-law Samuel Coleridge and Scottish poet/novelist Sir Walter Scott. Scott wrote most of *Marmion*, an epic poem about the Battle of Flodden (published 1808), whilst staying at 'Gundimore', the house of friend William Stuart Rose, on the shore at Mudeford, east of Sandhills. William (1775–1843) was the son of George Rose (who owned Sandhills) and a translater and poet, like Scott.

Captain Frederick Marryat's novel *Peter Simple* (1834) about a young British midshipman during the Napoleonic Wars is reputed by the family to be based on the life of Admiral George Vernon Jackson, of 'Verno', Christchurch. **Major General Sir Owen Tudor Burne** (1837–1909) was a soldier and writer. Whilst resident at Church Hatch (1903–09) he wrote his autobiography *Memories* (1907). He also wrote one of the Oxford Series of *Rulers of India* and was a regular contributor to *The Times*. **Sir Arthur Conan Doyle** (1859–1930) featured Christchurch Castle in his novel *The White Company*, set around 1365. He was a guest at Avenue Cottage, Stanpit. **Evelyn Sharp** (1867–1955) visited Mill House, Chewton Bunny, in 1912, when Marie Curie was staying there. She was a suffragette and author. *Requiem for a Wren* (1955) by **Nevil Shute** features *Headland Belle*, one of the ferries that still plies the harbour today. *Place Mill* (1962) by children's author **Barbara Softly** is a novel set in the time of the English Civil War.

One of our foremost travel writers **H. V. Morton** visited Christchurch in *In Search of England* (1927), taking tea in Church Street (lobster at 4:30) before visiting the Priory. **Bill Bryson** (*Notes from a Small Island* (1996)) visited Highcliffe Castle and walked along the beach to Mudeford, admiring the view of the Priory, before legging it into Christchurch along the road (Stanpit and Purewell).

The Priory's 39 misericords (mercy seats) range in date from mid-13th-century to early-16th-century. One is reputed to be a representation of Richard III as a hunchback and appears as an illustration in the biography by **Terry Breverton**, *Richard III – The King in the Car Park* (2013).

Music

Christchurch Gilbert and Sullivan Society formed in 1984 and first performed that September at the newly opened Regent Centre with *Iolanthe*. The set for Act 1 comprised six fir trees acquired from the Forestry Commission, such were its simple beginnings. The company has gone from strength to strength, with some 40 members and having performed all but two of the Gilbert and Sullivan operettas. September's show at the Regent Centre comprises four evening performances and a matinee.

Christchurch Priory held a major Music and Arts Festival in 2014 and it is hoped that this will become a regular feature. The Priory also offers a series of large-scale evening concerts on at least one Saturday each month, many taking place by candlelight. A variety of music is provided by choral societies, orchestras and ensembles. Each December there is a popular rendition of Handel's *Messiah*. The Priory Choirs total more than 50 skilled singers, and young people aged 7–18 are welcome to join. The Priory is also home to the Grange

The Priory organ is one of the finest pipe organs in the south.

Choral Society, established in 1961 from members of the Signals Research and Development Establishment (SRDE) with a membership of 130 or so. Organ recitals are held on Thursday lunchtimes (12:30), with the organ console moved to the front of the nave so the audience can see the performer. There are also celebrity organ concerts on Wednesday evenings during summer. Chamber music concerts take place in the intimate Lady Chapel on Thursday lunchtimes in August. (For details of all these see www.christchurchpriory. org/music.)

Highcliffe Castle is also a venue for music lovers, with indoor and outdoor concerts throughout the year.

Christchurch and District Band is a community concert band with over 40 members. **Christchurch Music Centre** started in the late 1960s, running two wind bands (junior, up to grade 3, and senior, grade 4 and above), plus percussion ensemble for children, with some support from adults. **Sessions Music and Heritage Club** is a weekly club for young people aged 12+ who love music (folk to rock), meeting in the Old School House, Lymington Road, Highcliffe, on Thursday from 5:30 pm. **Coda Music Centre**, a purpose-designed music facility, based in a former Victorian dairy farm in Chewton Farm Road, Walkford, offers care to people of all ages and disabilities through the use of music. **Highcliffe Youth Choir** meet at St Mark Primary School. The **La Nova Singers** is a Christchurch all-female chamber choir, formed in 2004, specialising in performing classical choral music. There is also a community choir and rock choir.

Famous past musicians associated with Christchurch include **Henry Francis Lyte**, cleric and hymn-writer (notably of *Abide With Me! fast falls the eventide* and *Praise My Soul the King of Heaven*); he visited Christchurch in 1837, his retired father then living in Purewell. **Sir Percy Florence Shelley** (1819–89), the son of poet Percy Bysshe Shelley and Mary Shelley, author of *Frankenstein*, sang at a Town Hall concert in 1860, which was presumably to mark the re-siting of the building in its current location in the High Street. Sir Percy's wife, Lady Shelley, also performed. **Sir Dan Godfrey** (1868–1939) was knighted for services to municipal music, having been Bournemouth Corporation's director of music for over 40 years; he lived at Amberwood House in Walkford.

Dance and Drama

There is a fair amount of 'drama' in Christchurch. **CADArts** holds a Performing Arts Festival annually, while **outdoor Shakespeare** takes place in the grounds of Priory House (with Bournemouth Shakespeare Players) and Highcliffe Castle. **Highcliffe Charity Players** was formed in 1971 from a group of local, mostly amateur actors. Their first pantomime was performed in St Mark's Church Hall the following year and performances are now held both there and at the Regent Centre.

Swish of the Curtain Theatre School is the south coast's leading part-time theatre school catering for children and young adults (2–20), with groups meeting at the Regent Centre and Twynham School. **Carousel Dance and Drama group** offers ballet classes for ages 3–8, held at Portfield Hall, as well as dance and drama for ages 4–10 at Christchurch Infants School, Addiscombe Road.

Film and TV

- Actor David Niven was billeted in Christchurch High Street during WW2.
- When *The First of the Few* (1942) was filmed, director/star Leslie Howard stayed in Christchurch. He played the role of R.J. Mitchell, designer of the Spitfire.
- Eric Morecambe was pictured pushing over a tower of pennies behind the Kings Arms bar *c.* 1966.
- Actor Stewart Granger was a regular visitor to Christchurch Airfield. His mother owned a property in Bournemouth until 1979.
- *The Duchess of Duke Street* (BBC) was a 1970s' series set between 1900 and 1925, telling the story of Rosa Lewis who ran the Cavendish Hotel in London. Rosa had formerly worked 'downstairs' at Highcliffe Castle.
- Consumer affairs programme *That's Life* (BBC) was filmed at Highcliffe Castle in 1974.
- Tommy Cooper visited *Tucktonia* in 1977, which had been reopened, following expansion, by Arthur Askey the previous year. *Tucktonia* was a 'Britain in miniature', built on the site of former Tuckton Golf School (which once boasted Britain's first floodlit course); it sadly closed in 1986.
- *The Famous Five*, an ITV series based on Enid Blyton's books, was filmed locally in 1978–79.
- Jon Pertwee visited Tucktonia when he was promoting *Worzel Gummidge*, which was on ITV (1979–81).
- The Rattenbury murder case (see Walk 5) was the subject of a play by Thomas Rattigan, and then a film *Cause Célèbre* (Anglia TV, 1987) starring Helen Mirren, Harry Andrews and David Suchet.
- *The Ruth Rendell Mysteries/Wexford* (ITV, 1987–2000), starring George Baker as the eponymous detective, did some filming at Highcliffe Castle.
- The 1990s' BBC series *One Foot in the Grave* was filmed partly in Christchurch, with both the Hospital and River Avon, close to Knapp Mill, featured in particular episodes. From series 2, exterior shots of the Meldrews' home were filmed at Tresilian Way, Walkford.

- *Songs of Praise* was filmed in the Priory in 1994. *Stars on Sunday* was also filmed there, with the Kings Arms used as a base for celebrities taking part.
- *Weekend Watch Dog – Live* (1997–2001), a spin-off from *Watchdog* (BBC), was filmed at Highcliffe Castle.
- *Heritage – Love It or Lose It* (*c.* 1998–2000) had episode 3 filmed at Highcliffe Castle.
- *The Real Kaiser Bill* (Channel 4, 1998), a documentary about Kaiser Wilhelm II, included filming at Highcliffe Castle.
- Guy Henry, who first appeared as a schoolboy member of Highcliffe Charity Players in the 1970s, went on to pursue a stage career with the RSC, also appearing as Pius Thicknesse in Harry Potter movies and Henrik Hanssen in BBC TV medical drama *Holby City* (first screened 1999).
- EastEnders actress Patsy Palmer was filmed at Highcliffe Castle as part of ITV's *Year of Promise* buildup to the Millennium.
- *The Way We Live Now* (BBC mini-series, 2001) starring David Suchet was partly filmed on the beach just below Highcliffe Castle. It was an adaptation of an Anthony Trollope novel set in the 1870s.
- *Antiques Roadshow* (BBC) hosted by Michael Aspel was filmed at Highcliffe Castle in 2007.
- *Catching the Impossible* (Channel 4, 2010) featured the Avon in the episode *Going against the flow*, with actor Bernard Cribbins catching a salmon for the camera.
- *Mr Selfridge* (ITV, 2013) tells the story of the American entrepreneur and founder of the famous department store, who was a tenant at Highcliffe Castle.
- *Invasion of the Job Snatchers*, a BBC documentary series screened in 2014 about getting young people into work, was filmed in Christchurch.
- Film star Hugh Grant was a visitor to the town at Easter 2014, eating in restaurants in Bridge Street (*Masala Bay*) and Church Street (*Splinters*).
- A German film of Rosamunde Pilcher's 1987 novel *The Shell Seekers* included filming at Highcliffe Castle in 2014.
- *Antiques Road Trip* (BBC) featured Christchurch in one episode in January 2015, including Bulstrodes auction house in Stour Road, close to the station, which was established in 1919. Antiques and Christchurch clearly go well together, as *Flog It!* came to Highcliffe Castle in June 2015.
- Two Priory School pupils, Oliver Payne and Finlay Wright-Stephens, appeared in the Oscar-winning film *The Theory of Everything* based on the life of Stephen Hawking. They are both members of Swish of the Curtain Theatre School.
- Diarmuid Gavin, of *Gardeners' World*, visited Stewarts in Somerford in April 2015, chatting with residents about plans for their own gardens and sharing his planting expertise.

The Regent Centre

At the heart of entertainment in the borough and an important part of its economy is the Regent Centre, a venue for arts, entertainment and the community in the middle of the High Street. Gary Theobald is responsible for press, publicity and film bookings.

> 'We are open 365 days a year, including Christmas Day, drawing people into the town from as far afield as Southampton, Dorchester and Weymouth. We have a rolling programme of improvements … whilst seeking to maintain the Art Deco heritage that gives people that experience of going back in time. We have 450-plus seats, so bigger than some modern multiplex auditoriums. We also look at the programme constantly to make sure we are putting on what people want, a variety of shows, everything from films and amateur dramatics to tribute acts and satellite broadcasts. Our image is certainly changing as we cater for a wider audience. We also act as box-office for other arts in the area, for example, Priory concerts.'

Christchurch became home to Dorset's smallest museum when a new attraction opened at the Regent Centre in July 2015. Measuring just 4.7×3.7 m, the cinema's museum is in the projection box on the roof of the theatre, which is now included in Regent Centre tours.

In 2000 a new Studio Theatre was opened at the rear of the Regent Centre, jointly funded by the Regent Centre Association and Council as the borough's main Millennium project.

Ivo the Clown

Entertainment takes many forms. Ivo the Clown is a well-known local personality and Christchurch's only clown.

> 'I came out of the RAF [in 1957], eventually moving into the milk trade. It was when we put on a Christmas party for children I realised I was a natural clown

(it's not something you can be taught) and I've never looked back. I'm a member of both Clowns International and World Clowns Association and my disabled son Carl is an honorary member of both, joining me on parades. It takes me half-an-hour to do make-up, which has to be as registered with Clowns International and is recorded on a china pot-egg, which is at the Clowns Museum / Exhibition at Wookey Hole, Somerset. Clowning has taken me around the world (you can laugh in any language), but Christchurch is as good a place as any to be a clown. The town appreciates me and I appreciate it in return. I feel I could walk into any establishment in Christchurch and be welcomed.'

Ivo in his trademark black cab is often seen at fetes, festivals, parades, children's parties, school and hospital visits, and doing in-store promotions.

Folklore and Strange Happenings

Things that Go 'Bump'

Christchurch has ghost stories too innumerable to detail in full, but here are some haunted places and their associated paranormal phenomena.

Ye Olde George Inn is allegedly haunted by a ghost known as 'the Grey Lady', whilst **Thomas Tripp** has the spirit of John Lovell, a former licensee. In Church Street's old **Castle Tavern** (now 'Soho') a strange mist was seen emerging from a wall, which then disappeared into the floor where the castle's ditch once was. Glasses have appeared to move off shelves, the figure of an old lady was

The George's Grey Lady has a penchant for throwing condiments off tables.

seen on the stairs, whilst a man in black and a small boy were also spotted, both vanishing when looked at. The ghosts appear to have vacated now that the modern restaurant and bar has moved in. Perhaps they don't like refurbishments.

The old Castle Tavern also has a few stories to tell.

In the High Street, **Woolworths** (now the 99p Store) had reports of figures walking through walls, strange noises and lights going on and off after closing time. The **Regent Centre** had a visitation in the mid-1980s from a ghostly couple in the stalls, with noises also heard behind the stage and objects moved. The **library** was reputedly visited by a grey lady in 1943, assumed to be Matilda Druitt, Herbert Druitt's mother, who had died that year, the library having once been the

Druitt family home. In **Bridge Street** a figure dressed in Civil War armour with his horse has been seen in a back garden, whilst ghostly pilgrims have been heard chanting and playing pipes and drums as they advanced over Town Bridge. The Priory was a pilgrimage site in the past because of its miraculous beam and the cures effected in or near the Priory, many for failing eyesight, possibly due to pure water in the area's wells and rivers.

At **Red House Museum** a former staff member believed the building to be haunted by various figures and reported hearing strange noises, unsurprising perhaps given the building's previous life as a workhouse. At **Place Mill** shapes have been seen on the first floor in the grain hopper. In Barrack Road the former **barracks** appear to have been 'visited' by a WW1 soldier in the 1970s, a figure being spotted on a first-floor corridor which vanished into its own cigarette smoke. There was apparently a sad case of a soldier taking his own life whilst detained at the barracks in WW1; whether this is connected or not, who can say. The figure was seen more than once, and another witness, a security supervisor, testified to the freezing temperatures he experienced in the same place.

The **Lighthouse Youth Centre** (formerly Stour Cottage) once housed an amusement arcade; there were stories of machines being moved about when the building was empty. At the hotel next to the **Bailey Bridge** inn, reputedly objects have moved in two bedrooms and doors have opened for no reason, whilst a cleaner felt a hand on her shoulder. Table settings have also been disturbed, with cutlery ending up on the floor in the inn. In Bargates, the **Conservative Club** has had reports of a female figure seen on the stairs and footsteps have been heard on the first floor. In the **Fusee Building** footsteps were heard on the first floor late in the evening when no one was up there.

Keep your eyes open if you visit **Highcliffe Castle** as there are ghost stories aplenty. There have been reports of doors opening and shutting, lights in a display case coming on again having been switched off and mysterious footsteps outside when no one was present. The figure of a woman has also been reported looking out from a window in the West Tower.

Stories Connected with the Priory

High among the easternmost arches of the nave (south side) is a mysterious stone-carved face known as 'Sam', believed to have been a Saxon workman or foreman employed on the building of the Norman church as he is flamboyantly mustachioed, as was Saxon fashion. His importance is unclear, but gazing at his face you could be staring at the likeness of one of the town's earliest inhabitants.

An old face in the Priory. (Courtesy of photographer Ross Whitehair.)

As you might expect from a building that is over 900 years old, the Priory has a few ghost stories to tell. The smell of frankincense was reported in the nave in the 1970s, although it would have been last used in 1539 prior to the Dissolution. Footsteps were heard in the quire aisle, described as sandals on a stone floor, even though it has a carpeted floor. Chanting has been reported when no services have been taking place. Figures have been 'experienced' both on the stairs leading to and in the doorway to St Michael's Loft. In 1999 an on-duty Priory official began mysteriously writing in old-French, having first heard a loud crash above his head. There have been reports of ghostly monks in the gardens, and a spectral monks' funeral procession witnessed by a former vicar on his way home to the vicarage. There have also been reports of a monk-like figure at the top of the tower staircase, whilst the Draper Chapel is allegedly visited by the eponymous John Draper, the last prior, who died in 1552. Mysterious tapping noises were reported in 1972 when restoration was in progress, but usually at weekends when workmen were absent (perhaps masons of old were helping out); there was also the mysterious opening of a door on the Priory's south side.

The old Porter's Lodge, the scene of Old Joe's hauntings.

In Priory House, which is only about 2 m from the Priory's south side, covers were violently pulled off the bed of an expectant mother. Priory Cottage (the old Porter's Lodge) has the ghost of 'Old Joe', a former verger at the Priory, although he hasn't been seen since the early 1950s.

The magnificent Salisbury Chantry in the Priory's north quire aisle was intended as Margaret, Countess of Salisbury's burial place. Unfortunately, the Countess fell foul of Henry VIII simply because she was a Yorkist and was beheaded in 1541, aged 67. Buried at the Tower of London, her beautiful chantry was never used.

The churchyard has a tomb chest with a fascinating inscription implying there are ten men buried there, 'not slayne, but raysd, raysd not to life, but to be buried twice, by men of strife … here we ten are one'. The date 1641, just before the English Civil War, and use of 'strife' suggest violence. It has been posited that the ten were shipwrecked, buried near the shore, then reburied in the churchyard. The 'men of strife' is a mystery; perhaps they were wreckers who lured a ship and its crew on to rocks? Poet Robert Southey recorded a local story that the men had been killed by a landfall whilst digging in a gravel pit, and another that they were Royalists dug up during the Civil War. We may never know.

During the Great Storm of November 1703, diarist John Evelyn recorded 4,000 great oaks falling in the New Forest. A hole some 10×4 m was blown in the stone slates of the Priory's nave roof. Christchurch was devastated, and 12 citizens lost their lives and were buried in the Priory graveyard.

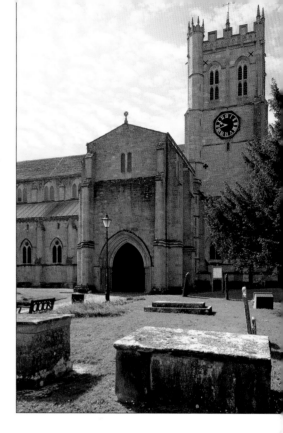

The grave of 'we ten' by the Priory's north porch and west tower.

Strange Creatures

The story goes that nine canons (priests) from Laon (France) visited Christchurch in 1113 on a fundraising tour for their cathedral which had been destroyed by fire. Thirty years later, retired Abbot Hermann wrote an account of their journey, including the earliest known description of Christchurch, where the canons reputedly encountered a five-headed, fire-breathing dragon. The most likely explanation is that they witnessed a meteorological phenomenon such as ball lightning, especially as Hermann's retelling states the weather was exceptionally stormy.

Mews Bridge, where Castle Street crosses the Mill Stream.

Then, in 1954 two local teenagers discovered a 60-cm-long crocodile close to Mews Bridge. It turned out the croc had been brought all the way from Hong Kong by a sailor on leave, had died, been buried on the river bank, then probably washed into the Mill Stream by heavy rain. If that wasn't enough, in 1971 five alligators from a touring circus escaped into the Stour. Fortunately they were recaptured, although one of them, a 2-m-long, one-eyed beast called Charlie, was at large for over a week.

Infamous Characters

It is said that the four knights who murdered Thomas à Becket in Canterbury Cathedral were granted sanctuary at the original Amberwood House in Walkford by Henry II.

Bure Homage in Bure Lane, Mudeford, was a splendid house owned in 1832 by former smuggler Sophie Dawes. She came from a poor fishing family, where her father topped up his income by smuggling. Sophie helped on these 'runs' and was allegedly a servant in a brothel, but in a rags-to-riches story she married into French aristocracy, becoming Baroness de Feuchères in 1818. She was alleged to have murdered her lover, the elderly Duc de Bourbon, in 1830 and, when acquitted, 'retired' to Bure Homage. Sadly the house was demolished for redevelopment in 1957; a lodge house still exists on Bure Lane, just north of Bure Homage Gardens, and the main house would have been behind this.

Bure Homage Lodge.

Is it possible that Jack the Ripper walked Christchurch's streets? The Druitt family were great benefactors to the town, bestowing their former properties – the buildings that are now Red House Museum and the library – to the town. But what of family member Montague Druitt? He was linked to the infamous 1888 Whitechapel murders and was mysteriously found drowned in the Thames shortly after the final murder.

There is a longstanding 'tradition' that Ethel Le Neve, secretary and mistress of notorious wife-killer Dr Crippen, lived and worked at Jumpers Corner Tea Rooms (now the Crooked Beam Restaurant) in the 1930s/40s. Bizarrely, what evidence there is now suggests the lady's identity was Lilian Vere, an eccentric, who may have impersonated Le Neve.

Family Fun and Other Activities

Here's what some youngsters have to say about living in Christchurch:

'It's an interesting, fun place to explore … [with] lots of things you can't do elsewhere.' (Honor Burgess)

'… there's a real community spirit, with lots done for charity … but [it] could advertise itself more, e.g. the sailing clubs are not well known.' (Anna-Marie Clay)

'It's quite quiet, which is nice … and there's lots of history. I live near a common, where I play football and also cycle on St Catherine's Hill and Hengistbury Head and have been in the swimming club at Two Riversmeet.' (Sam Cotton)

'I enjoyed Christchurch Quay when I was young and parks and open space, but now I'm a bit older I love to be around the town and shops. The history is good, as not everywhere has castles, although I think we should advertise more as an historical place.' (Luke Hewitt)

'I live in Mudeford and it's brilliant by the beach … There are good waves, which I taught myself to ride; just threw myself in. I've loved growing up here and I've never been bored. It's easy to get to places. The town could be adapted more for a younger generation, but, having said that, the Regent Centre is putting bands on … I went to Priory School so always had that link with the Priory, which is a lovely place to be. I could spend hours there; there is so much to see historically.' (Dan Mundy)

'I've done quite a bit of sailing in the harbour at Mudeford …. I've skateboarded at Two Riversmeet and used the football and biking since they opened. It is a good facility; always packed. The Priory brings tourists in and is increasingly relevant to and engaging with the young. I'm in the Priory Church Choir, so participate in Christchurch Priory's Music and Arts Festival, when we have lots of different classical music artists. I would like to be a singer-songwriter myself and have found great inspiration here.' (Ben Dunsford)

'Christchurch is a tight-knit community, which I'll be sad to leave. I want to be a writer and Christchurch gave me opportunities to get started. I never ran out of things to say when writing for Christchurch Eye, as there were always events going on. I've found the town welcoming and prepared to give you a chance.' (Grace Ball, former writer for the 'Teen Column' in Christchurch Eye magazine)

Play Areas

There are currently 28 children's playgrounds in the borough, so there is no shortage of places for youngsters to swing, slide and see-saw. **High 5 Play Park** (Highcliffe Recreation Ground, Lymington Road) includes an aerial cableway, overhead rotator, climbing zone, trim trail and ball court.

The **Splash Park** is an exciting water play park and paddling pool, which opened in 2010, replacing a traditional paddling pool, on Mayors Mead, adjacent to the Quomps on the Quay. Interactive features include water sprays, and the park is open April–September, automatically shutting down at 7 pm each evening.

Fun in the Splash Park. (Courtesy of photographer Allan Wood. © Christchurch Borough Council.)

There are **wheel parks** (for skaters, BMX, scooters and rollerblades) at Two Riversmeet and Waterman's Park; the latter is on Dorset Road, which can be accessed from Somerford Road.

Skate park and AstroTurf pitches at the Leisure Complex.

Opposite Bournemouth Airport on the former Merritown Farm site, Merritown Lane, Hurn, **Adventure Wonderland** is a *Primary Times* Star Awards-winning, family-run theme park aimed primarily at young children, with 30 rides and attractions included in the entry price. **Wild Thing!**

An award-winning theme park.

Mudeford Quay – a good place for crabbing.

is part of the set-up, a large Aztec-themed indoor play-centre with slides, climbing frames and 'Montyzoomers Thunderdome'. Opened as Alice in Wonderland Park in 1992, the park was rebranded Adventure Wonderland in 2005 when Wild Thing! opened. The whole place is open during summer (April–September), weekends in March and October, plus February half-term, with Wild Thing! also open through the winter.

Crazy golf is available at Tuckton Tea Gardens and The Boathouse, Christchurch Quay. **Crabbing** is a popular activity at Mudeford Quay, while the Bailey Bridge on Stanpit Marsh is a quieter spot.

Youth Centres and Groups

Christchurch Activities for Young People (**CAYP**) provides affordable activities for young people and families during school holidays, e.g. arts and crafts, cookery, sports and trips (see www.christchurchactivities.org.uk). In 2015 it was announced that some CAYP youngsters would participate in a new project exploring the science of water and the Harbour's peculiar double tide, and a science fair was held in Saxon Square to celebrate the project, attended by some 600 people.

Other places for young people are **Burton Youth and Community Centre** based at Sandy Plot and **Somerford Youth Centre** at Bingham Road, Christchurch. **Walkford Youth Club** was set up in 2010 and now has more than 400 children on its register. It runs two sessions a week in Ringwood Road, Walkford, and was presented with a meritorious award in 2015. The **Lighthouse Youth and Community Centre** on Barrack Road close to the recreation ground is open in the evenings for 13- to 19-year-olds to meet and participate in music, which is at the heart of the centre's activity. 'Lighthouse Live' is an annual weekend

The Lighthouse has a great atmosphere and is a safe centre for young people.

music festival put on by the teenagers, which takes place on the rear patio, spilling on to the adjacent rec.

The following quotes from Henry Weir-Parsons, Andrea Murphy, Elisse Bennett and Jess Cooper describe how they feel about Christchurch: '*a nice town*', '*less crowded and more peaceful*', '*with a good variety of shops*', somewhere '*I always feel safe*'. These comments suggest that today's youths value much the same qualities as older folk, and these teens singled out many places around the town for praise, including the Regent Centre, castle ruins, Quay where ducks are fed, Stompin' on the Quomps, library, ceramic café, Monday market (not always an option for those at school, of course), Red House Museum (which offers Family Explorer Days), ducking stool, and the Priory (with its guided walks). They even highlighted the volunteers and community spirit that keep things ticking over.

Scouting has been in Christchurch since 1908 and today offers nearly 600 local young people fun, friends and adventure. **Guides and Brownies** are represented by Bransgore & Burton, Christchurch, and Mudeford & Highcliffe Districts. Amanda Shorey of Mudeford has received the charity's highest accolade, the Queen's Guide Award, a feat achieved by only a handful of the organisation's half-million members annually.

Christchurch Sea Cadets is part of the UK's oldest nautical youth charity, giving youngsters the chance to go to sea, learn to sail and do adventure training. The winter HQ is Portfield Hall and summer HQ Christchurch Quay by the Rowing Club, handy for the harbour and Solent and with direct access to the Stour. Rowing, sailing, power-boating and kayaking are all offered.

Boating and Ferries

Bournemouth Boating rents out self-drive motor boats (maximum eight passengers) on an hourly basis from Tuckton Tea Gardens, Wick Ferry and Town Quay, and four-man rowing boats are available at the Tea Gardens.

Hire boats are only allowed on the river and in the harbour, exit to the sea being strictly prohibited.

Tuckton Tea Gardens are great for the kids, with crazy-golf and a putting green, only a short walk from Wick Ferry. Bournemouth Boating also offers barbecue cruises from here.

Quay Leisure operates from Town Quay, renting similar motor boats hourly as well. Boats can be hired between Easter and October and dogs are acceptable on board.

Mudeford Ferry runs between Mudeford Quay and the Sandbank from Easter to late October approximately every 15 minutes, and also

The Mudedford ferry makes its way down the harbour. (Courtesy of photographer Jake Moore. © Christchurch Borough Council.)

winter weekends, weather permitting. Bournemouth Boating offers a vintage ferry service from Tuckton Tea Gardens to Mudeford Sandbank from Easter to the end of October, as regularly as every 30 minutes, depending on weather and time of year. It also operates Wick Ferry across the Stour from Christchurch to Wick (Bournemouth) from Easter to the end of October, 10 am–5 pm. Passengers and dogs can be picked up from Town Quay, Wick Ferry and Tuckton Tea Gardens. The ferries use a class of boat known as *Headland* dating from the 1930s and constructed at Elkins Boatyard. Chris Wood is one of the ferrymen.

'I began as a student driving the ferries, then, when I retired in 2000, returned to the job I had loved. The four blue ferries (Headland Pal, Queen, Maid and Belle) date back to 1934. One of the reasons they've survived is they were unsuitable for wartime duties at sea due to their peculiar propulsion system and shallow draft, essential for working Christchurch Harbour. There used to be over 20 vessels on ferry duties, including rowing boats across the harbour. There was also an Isle of Wight ferry (Island Queen) which went from Pontins to Yarmouth and

carried around 100 passengers, the largest ferry using the harbour. Pontins used to generate a vast amount of traffic.

Today the Mudeford Ferry is the busiest, maybe due to the sandbank's popularity. Back in Victorian/Edwardian times people used to enjoy tea boats; now it's the café. There used to be a real community spirit in the old days when a lot of Southampton families owned beach huts. People arrived by train and boarded the ferry with cases. We even used to operate an early ferry, sailing upstream for Priory church services.

A group of Edwardian holidaymakers anchored in the Stour off Town Quay c. 1910. (© Hampshire County Council. Provided by Hampshire Cultural Trust.)

I've seen lots of changes. When I began back in the '60s there were few private vessels. All boats were wooden in those days, but the fiberglass, low-maintenance boats of today mean a lot more people have their own craft. A ferry of mine sank once. Someone had thrown an old water tank in the river, which I hit, punching holes in the boat. I had around 20 passengers on board, but we were only a few yards from Tuckton pontoon and they all got off without even getting their feet wet! People sometimes ask "Don't you get bored?" and the answer is "no". Every trip is different, with new passengers. Currents change and berthing can be difficult, especially with a prevailing south-westerly and ebb tide. It is a beautiful place to cruise, which I've come to appreciate more as I've got older.'

Town Quay and Wick Ferry pontoons are composed of redundant anti-submarine flotation tanks from WW2 (nets would have been suspended from these across the mouth of a harbour or naval base).

Sport and Leisure

Sailing

There are three sailing clubs in and around Christchurch. **Christchurch Sailing Club** is generally thought to date from 1874, with its first clubhouse built in 1896, although recreational sailing would have taken place in the harbour long before. Today the club has over 1,000 members, owning around 250 sailing dinghies and over 200 cruisers.

Highcliffe Sailing Club is located next to the RNLI on Mudeford Quay, its clubhouse named after the Sea Vixen airplane built for the Royal Navy at Christchurch's De Havilland factory.

Mudeford Sailing Club formed in 1961 and is based on the northeast shore of the harbour, adjacent to Stride's Moorings, about 200 m to the east of the end of Argyle Road, where it has a former Dutch barge, *Vrouwe Johanna*, acting as a clubhouse. Mudeford Week is a friendly, family-oriented regatta which takes place in the harbour in the first week of August.

Christchurch Yachting is a yacht charter operator (skippered or bareboat) based in the harbour, which also offers yacht tuition on owners' boats.

Christchurch Maritime Volunteer Service offers opportunities for all to enjoy the experience of boating and receive practical and theoretical training. Meetings are held on Monday evenings in the community room at the Fire Station, Fairmile Road.

Christchurch Sailing Club, a prime spot for watching the comings and goings on the river.

Christchurch-born **Pete Allam** won an Olympic bronze medal at the 1984 Los Angeles Games with Jonathan Richards in the 'Flying Dutchman' class. The dinghy was built at Bob Hoare's boatyard in Jumpers Avenue, Christchurch. The boatyard was also responsible for Rodney Pattison's gold-medal-winning boats in the same class (1968 and 1972). A bench-seat close to the Splash Park commemorates Christchurch's three medal-winning boats and was unveiled by Great Britain's most successful Olympic sailor, Ben Ainslie. Along the top of the seat is '*Supercalifragilisticexpialidocious*', the name of one of the boats. Pete Allam received a meritorious award from the Borough Council in April 2015.

Water Sports

Christchurch has endless opportunities for water sports. **Crazywater Surf School** operates from Highcliffe Beach, offering learn-to-surf and stand-up paddle boarding.

Between April and October, Nick May, owner of **Shore Sports Christchurch**, can be found at Mudeford Quay. Nick offers people of all ages the opportunity to learn kayaking, paddle boarding and windsurfing.

'*When I was a kid we came to Mudeford for holidays (my parents had a beach hut on the sand spit). Now I earn my living here, doing what I love. A lot of my customers came here on holiday, then moved here; it's that sort of place. The environment is perfect. With harbour, spit and rivers, it is one of the best locations in the country for watersports.*

The kayak tours are our most popular activity, with the one starting at Mudeford Quay, navigating the Avon's bridges, most booked. We do another up the Stour… Stand-up paddle boarding is the UK's fastest growing "craze" and is a cool activity, most popular with younger people in their 20s and 30s who want to have fun and stay fit. We have a real range of ages though, with school groups doing kayaking as well as people in their 70s. Our sports are easier than many suppose and therefore accessible to lots of people. We take safety very seriously and 99% of our activity is in the shallow harbour and rivers, keeping it safer.'

Christchurch Windsurfing Club also offers windsurfing, kitesurfing and paddle boarding from its clubhouse at Steamer Point. **Avonmouth Watersports** is a family-run sailing and watersports school based at Mudeford Quay, providing sailing and power-boating courses, as well as kayak, dinghy and windsurfer hire. If you feel the need for speed, **Adventure Voyages of Christchurch UK** has fast boats at Mudeford Quay and Sandbank offering Bay Blast and Needles tours daily in summer. **Blue Ride** offers RYA courses in RIB (rigid inflatable boat) and powerboat training in Christchurch Bay. Its training base is at Christchurch Rowing Club.

Adventure Voyages' 9-m RIB Sensation travels at speeds of 30 knots (35 mph) and lives up to its name.

Rowing

Christchurch Rowing Club was established in 1948. At the inauguration of the club, Mr Mead who presided was quoted as saying, 'If we are going to have a rowing club it must not only have a good reputation in Christchurch, but also all over England'. On its website is the tag-line 'Medals last longer than pain', so it seems to be living up to this sentiment. Its current clubhouse at Wick Lane next to the Captain's Club Hotel was built in the mid-1960s. The

A great place to see some action. If the door happens to be open, you can take a peek inside the boat store at the clubhouse.

club welcomes new members, both adult and junior (aged 12–18). 'The Head of the Stour' is held each March, a time-trial from Mudeford Sandbank to the clubhouse, a distance of around 2 miles, and the June Regatta sees many rowers take to the water.

Fishing

Fishing is part of Christchurch's story. Waters here are renowned for some of the best all-round fishing in the country, whether that be coarse, sea or game. Coarse fishing on the Avon's world-famous Royalty Fishery is excellent, with quality barbel, carp, roach, chub, dace and bream regularly caught. Salmon and sea-trout fishing is also available on a day-ticket at the Royalty. Sea fishing in the harbour at Stanpit is good for mullet and bass in spring and summer, whilst Mudeford offers all-year beach-casting.

Fishermen are often seen on the River Avon below Town Bridge.

Davis Fishing Tackle, 71–75 Bargates, sits on the corner of Avon Buildings and the entrance to the Royalty Fishery. Morris and Mona Davis set up a stationer's business here in 1945 but were encouraged to stock fishing tackle, and in no time the stationery had gone and they had 50 biscuit tins of maggots arriving at Christchurch Station every week. Nigel and Helen Gray bought the business in 2004 and take up the story.

'We're the only fishing shop in Christchurch and have customers from all over the globe, as well as locals. We receive orders from the likes of Russia, Japan and Canada, plus people coming to use the Fishery, for example, from Australia and New Zealand. Some 5,000 fishermen use the Royalty each year and the business

Davis Fishing Tackle has been a fixture in the town since 1945.

is worth £5 million to Christchurch's economy. Sometimes we have 30 people queuing on the pavement at 7:30 in the morning, such is its popularity. We've had to expand from the original premises into two next door, but deliberately kept the old shop as it was. Our customers like it that way and some of them bring grandchildren in to see the "Emporium" as they call it. The Royalty is open for coarse fishing throughout, except during the close season – March 15th to June 16th – when it is open for salmon fishing, which means a later start.'

Christchurch Angling Club dates to 1938 and is one of the UK's longest established angling clubs, with over 35 waters on its book. Well-known waters, exceptional fish and a friendly club atmosphere have made this an ongoing success story. Waters include some of the best stretches of the Dorset Stour and Hampshire Avon, with many places to fish 'off the beaten track'. The club plays a major part in habitat upkeep, as well as coaching and education, with young anglers being an important part of the membership.

Football

Christchurch Football Club (established 1885) played for years at Barrack Road Recreation Ground in the town centre, before moving to the picturesque setting of Hurn Bridge in 1984. The club has played in the Wessex League since 1987. In its early days it had a nickname of *Can't Whack 'Ems*, such was the club's invincibility.

Jody Craddock began his career at Christchurch FC, a veritable 'rags to riches' story that saw him play Premiership football at Sunderland and Wolverhampton.

Hurn Bridge, the home of Christchurch football and cricket.

'I played two seasons at Christchurch (1992/93), a 17- to 18-year-old in the 1st Team. I was always a central defender and my time at Christchurch brought my game on. I had a trial at Cambridge United, staying there 4 years, before moving to Sunderland (6 years) and Wolves (10 years). I gained promotion to the Premiership with both clubs and enjoyed massive derby games against Newcastle and West Bromwich, which were so important to fans and players. One of my biggest disappointments was the 1998 play-off final with Sunderland, when we lost 7–6 to Charlton on penalties in front of over 77,000 fans at Wembley.

I wouldn't say I was one of the most naturally gifted players, but I made up for that with passion and determination. I worked hard, tried improving and was fortunate to remain relatively injury free, which prolonged my career. I played the professional game for 20 years and played in an honest way; in well over 500 appearances I was never sent off. The start I had at Christchurch was a big influence. It was a club with a family feel and we were always able to play on a nice pitch, which is important to a player. Playing in the First Team at such a young age taught me to look after myself on the pitch, toughened me up and gave me the grit and determination needed to forge a career.'

The club has U-8 to U-16 youth teams, whilst the U-18 side competes in the FA Youth Cup. Other youth football teams include Burton Youth and Highcliffe Hawkes, and ladies and girls are represented by Mudeford Phoenix.

Famous former footballers who now live in Christchurch include Bob Wilson (Arsenal and Scotland) and Ron 'Chopper' Harris (Chelsea).

Cricket

Christchurch Cricket Club has a long history, as illustrated by the 1871 defeat of the Royal Horse Artillery Christchurch Barracks, a reminder also that the military had its off-duty moments. The club shares Hurn Bridge Sports Ground with Christchurch FC, with senior teams playing in both Saturday and Sunday Dorset Leagues. The junior section covers the U-9 to U-16 age ranges. Dorset Cricket Centre is also based here, offering year-round facilities for indoor training.

Mudeford Cricket Club (established in 1848) plays home games in a delightful village setting on Stanpit (road), just under half-a-mile from Purewell roundabout.

Famous West-Indian cricketer Sir Learie Constantine visited the town in 1964 to open a new nurses home at Christchurch Hospital (Trinidad House). Constantine took the first West Indian Test wicket and was also a lawyer and politician who became the UK's first black peer in 1969.

Golf and 'Footgolf'

Christchurch Golf Club is based at Iford, next to the River Stour, where there are two courses: the par-72 parkland Bridge Course and the smaller 9-hole, par-3 Stour Academy course. It was set up in 1977 by a group of local men who wanted to make golf club membership accessible to those not having an official handicap. Ryder Cup star Colin Montgomerie was a shareholder in the original company. The course expanded over the river in 2001 and the club now has a 60-bay, two-tier driving range.

Highcliffe Castle Golf Club has sea glimpses through a beautiful tree canopy surrounding the 18-hole, par-64 parkland course. The original 9-hole course was opened in 1913 by Queen Victoria's third daughter Princess Helena and her daughter Princess Victoria within the grounds of the castle. WW1 air ace Major W.R. Read used to land his plane on the golf course. It is believed the club holds a British record for the oldest person to make a hole-in-one: Mr T.S. South achieved this in 1952, aged 91. Cecil Sargent was the longest-serving pro at any club in the world, serving as assistant-pro, then pro for 57 years (1917–74). Cecil was wounded at the Somme in WW1 and discharged from the army, as was a previous pro, Albert (Percy) Percival, who lost some fingers in the fighting. Despite this, Albert was a respected club-maker, producing clubs at his own premises in Seaton Road, Highcliffe.

Pay and play golf is available at Two Riversmeet Leisure Complex and Dudmoor Farm, below St Catherine's Hill. Parley Golf Centre, opposite the airport, offers a 27-bay driving range and 9-hole course. Its 'Sand Wedge' café bar is open to all. All courses are open to visitors, although you will need to be a member of an affiliated golf club in order to play at Highcliffe.

The golf course at Two Riversmeet has also been adapted to be used as a footgolf course. Footgolf, one of the fastest growing sports in the UK, has the same philosophy as golf, but players kick a football to try to achieve or better their score on the new and improved 9-hole golf course. Having the two courses means families can play together, parents thwacking golf balls and children launching footballs!

Bowls

Christchurch Bowling Club, which began in 1925, no longer exists; due to a declining membership it played its last game on the green opposite the Kings Arms in 2013. It is believed that a green existed here since the late 18th century, when it was used for both bowls and croquet. The club's former premises are now owned by the Kings Arms, with the Pavilion used as a wedding venue.

Bowling at New Meadows.

Outdoor bowling at Highcliffe Bowling Club occurs in the beautiful setting of Nea Meadows, a local nature reserve, and at Iford Bridge Bowling Club. Indoor bowling is the preserve of East Dorset Indoor Bowls Club, the first purpose-built indoor bowling club in the area, adjacent to Two Riversmeet. Pay-per-session bowling is available at Highcliffe. East Dorset is a members club; however, there are 'free play sessions' from time to time for non-bowlers or those thinking of taking up the sport. Iford Bridge is a members club.

Tennis

Christchurch Tennis Facility has four pay-and-play hard tennis courts, two of which are floodlit, at the Iford Sports Complex. Mudeford Wood Tennis Club has around 70 members, three synthetic-grass all-weather courts and floodlighting at Mudeford Wood Community Centre on Pipers Drive.

Athletics

Christchurch Runners meet at the East Christchurch Sports and Social Club in Grange Road. Originally formed as a works club for Plessey in 1982, it is now open to all and currently has around 50 members. Everyone is welcome, no matter what your standard, and if you don't fancy running there is always the option of time-keeping.

Swimming

A beach segregation scheme exists, with designated bathing beaches at Avon Beach and Friars Cliff, Highcliffe Castle and Mudeford Sandbank. Two Riversmeet has a 25-m main pool and 12.5-m training pool and is home to Seagulls Swimming Club, offering competitive swimming, water polo and synchronised swimming. Seabrook Seals is an open-water swimming group based in Christchurch and Bournemouth.

Horse Riding

Riding lessons (private and group) are available for all abilities at Dudmoor Farm. 'Walking treks' (on horseback) are offered on the heathland of St Catherine's Hill; suitable for beginners, these offer an introduction to riding, with no 'road work', as well as the chance to see some wildlife in a pleasant, lesser known part of the borough. Children's pony days run in the holidays,

A wide selection of ponies are available for all abilities at Dudmoor Farm.

offering both a long lesson and the chance to spend time with ponies, learning how to look after them.

Though no longer an event, Christchurch Races used to take place up until 1928 in a field between Stanpit and Somerford at Easter. These were held to Pony Turf Club rules, which regulated the racing of horses under 15 hands in the UK between 1923 and 1950.

Snowtrax

Snowtrax Alpine Activity Centre at Hurn offers skiing, snowboarding, ringos ('doughnuts') and ski-bob. Whether improving your skills or looking for lessons to get started, everyone is welcome at Christchurch's taste of the Alps (in fact it was the 'Alpine' setting that encouraged

Snowtrax, where you can learn to ski in a day.

Snowtrax to come here). If it all looks a tad too energetic, you can just relax in the Alpine Bar with its outside terrace and watch everyone else. There is also an Alpine Adventure Park with trampolines, swings and a huge fort. Snowtrax is not far from the airport; look out for the brown tourist signs with the skier.

Shooting

Christchurch Gun Club formed in 1902, moved to its current location on St Catherine's Hill in 1968 and now has over 500 members of all ages. Full-bore, military and sporting rifle, black powder and clay-pigeon shooting are all catered for. There is also an airgun gallery and woodland range. New members are welcome, with tuition and support available. There is a guest day on the second Sunday of each month, when visitors are welcome to come and see what takes place there.

Rugby Union

Christchurch no longer has its own rugby club. Former Christchurch Rugby Club members used to play on a pitch behind The Manor country-house hotel on Salisbury Road in Burton, and one notable team member was Michael (Mike) Wheeler, who won a bronze medal for Great Britain in the 4×400 m relay at the 1956 Melbourne Olympics.

Bournemouth Rugby Club plays at the 26-ha Chapel Gate site next to the airport, which hosts the biggest rugby 7s tournament in the world and is also a multisports venue, with archery, cricket, shooting, hockey, squash, football, golf and table tennis.

Two Riversmeet Leisure Complex

Paul Rutter became the general manager of Two Riversmeet Leisure Complex in February 2000 and is now Leisure Services Manager for Christchurch and East Dorset Partnership. The centre is a council-owned facility, with swimming, squash, badminton, martial-arts, a fitness suite, Wheel Park, skatepark, 3G synthetic ('Astro') football pitches and golf course. Paul, a Dorset boy, has always worked in the leisure industry and has presided over considerable changes at the centre.

> '... there has been a big boom in fitness the last 15–20 years, which is still growing. We consult with local public and users, so when the gym facility doubled, we installed equipment we knew people would use. Our 18-hole golf course has changed to 9-hole, as this fits better in the space and presents a more challenging course with larger greens. We've also seen the floodlit Wheel Park and BMX circuit occupy what was an empty space in 2005 and the 3G football pitches came on board in 2009.

The BMX park at Two Riversmeet reflects the close association of BMX with the sport of motor cross.

> Customers are predominantly Christchurch people, although 3G pitches bring in people from further afield, as they are high standard. Individual fitness and well-being is an important solo activity here, hence the gym facility has grown from a modest affair in the late '80s to 50 individual "stations", each with bike,

treadmill, etc. The recession has not seen any decline in use, in fact the contrary, as we've actually been busier, which shows we're offering facilities people want at affordable prices. We also have a good mix of users, which means the centre is utilised all day. During the day we have retired customers, then children early evening, followed by working adults. We have people in their 70s and 80s coming to play badminton!'

Other Facilities

As well as the Two Riversmeet fitness suite, Christchurch has the following gyms and personal trainers:

- Chi Kung exercise classes (Wessex Health, 17 Stour Road)
- Curves women's gym (4 Wilverley Road)
- Haynes personal training (12 Avon Wharf, Bridge Street)
- Mike Simms personal training and pilates (Shelley Close)
- Pilates Exercise Men and Women (242 Barrack Road)
- Urban Health and Fitness (71a High Street)
- Women's Workout (22 High Street)

There is also spa and gym membership available at Christchurch Harbour Hotel.

January 2015 saw ex-Twynham School pupil Scott 'Scotty Dog' Mitchell crowned British Darts Organisation World Champion at Frimley Green in Surrey. Scott immediately vowed to spend a sizeable chunk of his £100,000 winnings on a new tractor for the family farm at Ripley in the New Forest (just outside Christchurch).

Regular Events

Fairs and Markets

Christchurch used to have two fairs a year in medieval times: Trinity Fair in May/June, dating back to at least 1140, and St Faith's Fair in October, believed to have started in 1258. The last of these fairs was held in 1871.

First mention of a town market is in a charter dated 1150, although it may go back possibly to Saxon times, as the town became a fortified burgh under King Alfred; as well as being defended, Christchurch would have acted as a commercial and administrative centre. The market lapsed in Victorian times, to be revived in its current form in 1976.

Today the popular Monday market has roughly 50 stalls occupying the High Street and Saxon Square (the latter benefitting from a £3 million makeover in 2014). There is also a farmers' market on Fridays in Saxon Square, plus a Friday Craft Fair and Table Top Sale in the Druitt Hall. A new market showcasing local talent started in June 2015 (the second Sunday of the month) in the High Street, selling a variety of art, design, antiques and vintage wares.

Market-day in Saxon Square.

February

Shrove Tuesday pancake race – Christchurch Food and Wine Festival organises this charity event in Church Street, when 'individual chefs' and teams of four participate along an improvised race track on the cobbles.

May

Christchurch Food and Wine Festival, conceived as a Millennium one-off event, was so successful it has become the town's premier regular event, attracting around 70,000 visitors. Self-funding, it is organised by a small, diverse committee but wouldn't happen without volunteers. Chairman Vicki Hallam says:

> *'The festival has evolved into a street market, cooking demonstrations in a marquee and entertainment in Saxon Square, so there is something for everyone. We particularly want to get children involved, so have an Education Trust which promotes culinary skills in the young, a balanced diet and involves youngsters*

Showcasing the town and highlighting local producers at the Food and Wine Festival. (Courtesy of photographer Allan Wood. © Christchurch Borough Council.)

in cooking competitions, the finals of which are judged in our marquee. As well as the Trust the festival supports one other chosen charity annually. We don't charge for the festival but hope to receive donations, which help our charities, with profits going towards next year's festival. … When we started there were no other food festivals in the south, but others have followed Christchurch's success, modelling their events on us, which is a compliment to what we've achieved.'

Highcliffe Revival Food Festival has been organised to run in association with the Christchurch event, one of the initiatives of the Highcliffe Centre Partnership which aims to revitalise Highcliffe and its High Street.

PDSA Funday – including a dog show on Christchurch Quay.

June

Christchurch Regatta – first held in 1909, it organises some 70 races over a 1,200-m course on the River Stour between the Sailing and Rowing Clubs.

The Regatta, 20 August 1913. A starting pistol is fired for a swimming event. (© Hampshire County Council. Provided by Hampshire Cultural Trust. Photographer Moss.)

Highcliffe Summer Fayre – at St Mark Primary School.

Mudeford Wood Family Fun Day – at Mudeford Wood Community Centre.

Highcliffe Castle Shakespeare – plays performed outdoors late-June to mid-July.

July

Christchurch Music Festival – a weekend of live music and dance centred on the Quay, with live performances in some town-centre pubs.

Open-Air Shakespeare – performed in the garden of Priory House.

Mudeford Arts Festival – on Mudeford Quay Green, with local artists and craftmakers exhibiting, demonstrating and selling.

Funfair – for 2 weeks at the end of July/beginning of August on Barrack Road Recreation Ground.

August

Stompin' on the Quomps. (Courtesy of photographer Adrian Dwyer, www.photoworks.co.uk.)

Stompin' on the Quomps – on Town Quay; established in 1994, it is one of the largest 'smooth jazz' festivals in the south.

Christchurch Carnival – with a parade through town, displays and activities on the Quay, music, funfair and fireworks.

Mudeford Lifeboat Funday, where all profits support the local RNLI station and lifeguards. (Courtesy of photographer Jake Moore. © Christchurch Borough Council.)

Mudeford Lifeboat Funday – all proceeds from this event go to the Lifeboat Station. There are displays, a raft race, stalls, funfair, raffle and BBQ.

Duck Race – on August Bank Holiday, some 2,500 plastic ducks race down the Mill Stream, with a prize for the 'sponsor' of the winning duck. All money collected goes to Christchurch Lions Club local causes.

Classic Cars on the Quay – around the end of August/beginning of September, a static display on the Quomps of classic pre-1983 cars and bikes.

September

Fit Christchurch Family Fun Day – on Christchurch Quay, aiming to exhibit and promote healthy lifestyle choices, with displays and opportunities to try out products, activities and food.

November

Remembrance Sunday – wreath laying at Purewell Cross war memorial, followed by a parade from the Royal British Legion (Bargates) to the Priory, where further wreath laying precedes a church service. In the afternoon another wreath laying takes place at Highcliffe's war memorial, followed by a service in St Mark's.

Christmas Festival – on the last Saturday in November/first Saturday in December, a Christmas market in the High Street, with performances, arrival of Father Christmas and switching on of the lights.

Turning on the Christmas lights. (Courtesy of photographer Allan Wood. © Christchurch Borough Council.)

Interesting Buildings and Businesses

The Priory

The Priory is the town's most iconic building. A Saxon church existed here and after that a Norman one, as evidenced by the nave which dates to 1094. Founder Ranulph Flambard endured a stint in the Tower of London for over-enthusiastic tax collecting, but escaped after managing to get his guards thoroughly inebriated.

We owe the survival of the Priory church, the longest in the country, to last prior John Draper. Although the monastery was dissolved in 1540, Draper persuaded Henry VIII that the church should be saved for the townsfolk. The unfinished parapet on the roof of St Michael's Loft is due to the monks' sudden eviction.

The mighty north porch has a fascinating past – over the years it has been used for weddings, as a town hall, 'garage' for the town's ducking stool, and to house a whirly-gig and fire engine (these things were only dragged out when needed).

The Priory is still at the heart of the community over 900 years on. Although it is an ancient building, it has a modern community and there is a lot going on behind the scenes to move the parish forward. Attendance at special events (e.g. Remembrance and Christmas) is buoyant, although, as elsewhere, the stalwart congregation is falling. The Priory is looking to fully engage with families and people of working age, and there is a 'vision'

St Michael's Loft, formerly used as a school and now a museum.

for this building, with today's 'custodians' securing the church for future generations.

Reverend Canon Charles Stewart took up the position of Priest-in-Charge in Easter 2015. Plans for a new visitor centre and refectory, attached to Priory House, demonstrate that the Priory is not standing still. The extension will open up new views of the Priory, provide a more suitable museum space and enlarged shop, and will benefit both the Priory and the community.

Mike Beams, a retired Chartered Engineer and former churchwarden, is a volunteer responsible for the Priory's fabric, its two daughter churches (St George's at Jumpers and St John's at Purewell) and other parish buildings. In response to the question whether Mike is ever referred to as 'Miraculous Beams', he replies:

'I'm not very miraculous, but I do get called it sometimes. … In 2000 we began external conservation, cleaning and replacing stonework, which had not been done since Victorian times. We are about halfway round but need a further £2 million to complete the job. The place would eventually fall down if work is not done. The north quire aisle wall is leaning, as we found buttresses were not supporting the building which was erected on a graveyard. It hasn't fallen down yet!

Once the outside is done, the inside will need looking at. On top of that the Priory costs £1,200 a day to run. Its value is shown though by the 100,000 visitors we get annually, many overwhelmed by the interior. We have a largely Norman nave and a Perpendicular east-end, but all church building periods are represented. I think the greatest enigma we have is the stone Jesse Screen, which somehow survived the Puritan period, which I believe is fairly unique. I can show you lots of other statues that had heads knocked off. The miraculous beam gets more attention of course. This was on the floor in Victorian times, but people kept removing fragments as "relics". The North Porch is where the Prior used to meet his tenants when this was a working monastery. Today the Priory has a large number and variety of community uses, everything from craft fairs to school carol concerts.'

Priory House and Vicarages

Impressive Priory House, south of the Priory, was built by Gustavus Brander in 1776. Brander was a director and governor of the Bank of England, fellow of the Royal Society, Trustee of the British Museum and Lord of the Manor of Christchurch Twynham. He almost came to a watery end when his coach and horses bolted for the Thames in London in 1768. His fortunate escape led to him donating £200 to the Priory, and a sermon of gratitude was preached on the third Sunday in August (known locally as 'Coach and Horses Sunday'),

Priory House was purchased by public subscription in 1934 and is used for church functions and cultural and community events.

which still occurs. Brander died in 1787 and his will provided for the first organ for the Priory Church. Priory House was built on the site of the demolished cloister, lost at the Dissolution, and is just 1.8 m from the Priory's south side. Whilst uncovering remains of demolished monastic buildings, Brander found a concealed cache of bird bones, which may hint at an earlier pagan use of this site.

Christchurch unusually has two vicarages: as the 17th-century, Grade II-listed, nine-bed vicarage in Quay Road became too costly to maintain, a new four-bed vicarage was built in the garden, facing Church Street. This opened for use in March 2014.

The old vicarage (left), before conversion to apartments, and new one (above): two generations of vicarages.

Christchurch Castle

The town's castle was a classic Norman motte (mound) and bailey (courtyard) design, with the former bowling green occupying the bailey. It twice saw action: during the 12th-century civil war between Stephen of Blois and Empress Matilda and then during the 17th-century English Civil War, when it was captured by Parliamentarians and slighted on Cromwell's orders. The moat was filled in and buildings in Church Street and back gardens in Castle Street now occupy this site. Some of the iron-stone, originally from Hengistbury Head, ended up as foundations for the George Inn up the road. Today the castle is owned by English Heritage. The castle mound with remains of the keep on top can be accessed off Castle Street (no charge).

Constable's House

Constable's House abutting the Mill Stream was built in the 12th century for the Lord of the Manor's Constable (bailiff) and provided comfortable accommodation for important visitors. The building had walls up to 2.7 m thick. It was ransacked for stone in the 18th century but saved by Rev William Jackson, although it was still an ivy-clad ruin in 1910. It was donated to the town by Charlotte Druitt in the 1950s, with the ivy then being removed. Today's ruin includes a water gate and remarkable Norman chimney and flue, which make it stand out from the rugged Castle remains on the mound.

Constable's House was a house fit for visitng kings.

Place Mill

Place Mill (the 'place where the rivers meet').

The Grade II-listed watermill on Town Quay is mentioned in *Domesday* and once belonged to the Priory but ceased working in 1908. It is unique in taking water from one river (the Avon), via the specially constructed half-mile Mill Stream, to another (the Stour). A medieval stone bridge (Place Mill Bridge) crosses the Mill Stream close to the mill.

Highcliffe Castle

Magnificent Highcliffe Castle, built in the 1830s by Charles Stuart (Lord Stuart de Rothesay, former British Ambassador in Paris), is the second stately home to have been built here. The first, High Cliff Mansion, built by de Rothesay's grandfather, ex-Prime-Minister John Stuart, 3rd Earl of Bute, was abandoned in the early 19th century due to cliff erosion. The imposing white entrance

A large amount of medieval French masonry was used in the Castle's construction and the Gothic Revival-style architecture makes it look older than it is. A family home until the 1950s, then gutted by fire, it has been beautifully restored. (Courtesy of Highcliffe Castle. © Christchurch Borough Council.)

lodges of the Mansion were re-used for Highcliffe Castle and now form part of the Lord Bute hotel and restaurant complex. Medieval stone for the second castle was shipped across from France in steamers (hence the name 'Steamer Point'), one steamer being used as a site office and later a retreat. Charles Stuart was sufficiently wealthy to provide 'plate' (dishware and cutlery made of precious metal) plus liveried servants for the Duchess of Richmond's Ball, held 3 days before the Battle of Waterloo and dubbed 'the most famous ball in history'.

Between 1916 and 1921 Harry Gordon Selfridge (famous for his department store in London) rented the Castle and reputedly spent £25,000 on renovations (around £1 million today). When the US joined the War in 1917, his wife Rose opened a tented retreat (the 'Mrs Gordon Selfridge Convalescent Home for American Soldiers') in the grounds.

The castle was purchased by Christchurch Borough Council in 1977 in order to prevent further deterioration. Former actor, stage manager and Regent Centre manager David Hopkins has been manager there for over a decade.

'It is a case of "the phoenix flies", for the castle was a ruined shell following two calamitous fires in the 1960s. Some favoured conservation, others demolition, and the castle could easily have been lost. It has risen again, though, as the council has committed to the castle's improvement since the 1990s. A lot has been achieved, but there is much more to do. Future plans include a dedicated heritage centre, enabling a permanent display of internationally important 12th- to 16th-century stained glass, reinstatement of the elegant double staircase in the Great Hall, and roof terrace above the Winter Garden. We are the present custodians of this great treasure and history will judge how well we looked after it.

The kids love the tales of royal visitors – six kings/future kings, ten queens/future queens – including Edward VII and Kaiser Wilhelm II of Germany. Other famous visitors included Prime Minister William Gladstone, Australian-born soprano Nellie Melba and best-selling author Nancy Mitford. The children can't believe these royal figures actually stayed here, in Highcliffe, and that one of its most famous tenants was none other than American tycoon Harry Gordon Selfridge ("Mr Selfridge" fame). It is not all about history though. When I became manager I had not been here before and the place took my breath away with potential. We want to open up the whole 14-acre site to benefit the community and touch as many lives as possible with this fascinating story.'

The Kings Arms

The Kings Arms served as an assembly room for aristocracy coming to Christchurch for bathing and was listed in *Bradshaw's Handbook* of 1863

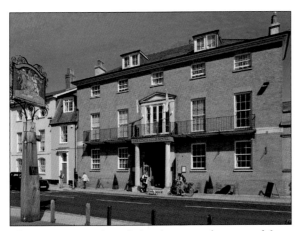

(a famous early railway guide of where to stay and what to see). Built by George Rose MP at the start of the 19th century, it became customary for newly elected MPs to throw ha'pennies from the balcony to children in the street. Notable guests include the 1st Duke of Marlborough and Winston Churchill. The hotel is in a prominent position in the heart of town, across the road from the castle ruins. There used to be tennis courts opposite laid out for guests and a croquet lawn, but by 1925 these had gone, replaced by the bowling green with a pretty clubhouse erected in 1988 (now a wedding pavilion). An annual flower show was held in the grounds where the hotel also used to have its tea garden. Lukasz Dwornik is the current manager.

The Kings Arms, the only hotel in town for most of the last 200 years.

'The Kings Arms has 20 varied rooms, including ones at the front with views of the castle and those overlooking a quiet courtyard at the rear. We have characterful rooms to suit every taste: high ceilinged rooms; interconnected ones with balcony; traditional wooden beams; loft rooms. In May 2013 we opened the Pavilion as a wedding venue and this is proving popular already, with couples coming from far afield to marry in the unique setting of a refurbished bowls clubhouse in the shadow of Priory and castle. Afterwards they can adjourn to the Kings Priory, our light and airy reception venue next to the hotel. People are drawn to the hotel by its restaurant, which gained a prestigious Michelin "Bib Gourmand", a mark of high-quality cuisine, good service and value for money and the only one in Dorset. All food served in the restaurant is sourced from within 15 miles.*

*Interestingly not all guests are tourists. We get many local people using the restaurant and booking a room to enjoy a mini-break. They also use the spa at sister hotel the Christchurch Harbour Hotel. We value the place of the Kings Arms at the heart of the community and we're more successful using local food, suppliers and supporting local businesses, as these things matter to people. We've worked with the Regent Centre, for example, to put on pre-show dinners and also have our own paper, The Kings Herald, telling people about events and offers. We ran a very successful one-off event in the old tea gardens, which became a real local occasion attended by some 450 people, so this is something we'd like to see happen regularly.'

Christchurch Barracks

Little remains to show for 200 years or so of Christchurch Barracks, with a retail park and housing now occupying the site (the original stable/barrack block and officers' mess have been converted to flats). Work began on the barracks in the Portfield (an area of Common now largely built over) in 1792 to accommodate half a troop of light cavalry, who arrived in 1795, their main purpose being to resist a threatened Napoleonic invasion. Troops would go on to fight in the Peninsular War, at Waterloo (one of its most distinguished officers was Sir Augustus Simon Frazer who commanded the Horse Artillery there), the Crimean War, Boer War and both World Wars.

The extant Grade II-listed guardroom (now a hairdressers) was built in 1811 and was the scene of a tragedy during WW2 when one sentry accidentally shot another. Its square turret, clock face, cupola and weathervane make this a familiar landmark along Barrack Road.

The former guardroom of the barracks.

A plaque and section of bridge sit on grass across from the Bailey Bridge pub-restaurant on Barrack Road.

At the Military Engineering Experimental Establishment (MEXE) here, the famous Bailey Bridge, which helped to shorten WW2, was invented under eponymous mastermind Sir Donald Bailey, who lived at 1 Twynham Avenue between 1946 and 1964. The barracks benefitted the local economy until closing in 1995 but are still remembered in the name

Brigadier Jarrett-Carr, the Duke of Edinburgh and Sir Donald Bailey outside the officers' mess at the MEXE c. 1970. (© Hampshire County Council. Provided by Hampshire Cultural Trust.)

Barrack Road, plus modern Lancer Close and Hussar Close. Two blocks of Liberty Court occupy some of the former parade ground.

Bournemouth Airport

The airport opened as RAF Hurn in 1941 and was home to Spitfires, Wellingtons and Typhoons, as well as being a base for some US squadrons. By 1945/46 it had become the country's main airport for foreign flights, until Heathrow opened; in fact, it was briefly Britain's only intercontinental airport, with flights to Accra, Cairo, Calcutta, Johannesburg, New York, Sydney and Washington DC. The airport became heavily involved in aircraft production (Vickers Viscounts, BAC 1-11s and components for Concorde). In 1958 the first Palmair flight took off from Hurn for Palma, Majorca; the Bournemouth-based company still operates from the airport today. Extension of the runway in 1995 saw Concorde fly in the following year, and in 2010 a new departures terminal was opened, with a new arrivals terminal the following year. The airfield, within the borough of Christchurch, was rebranded Bournemouth International and is now simply called Bournemouth Airport. It is an important part of the local economy.

The Railway Station

Although the current station west of Bargates dates to 1886, its predecessor was built in 1862 and celebrations to mark 150 years took place in 2012 . The station has always been an important gateway to the town, bringing thousands of holidaymakers to Wick Ferry Holiday Camp (Pontins). There are two platforms serving stations between London Waterloo (under 2 hours away) and Weymouth.

During WW2 the station was blacked out, with name boards removed and a policeman and porter checking IDs. Poignant pictures were taken leading up to D-Day, when the car park was packed with American GIs en-route to New Forest airfields and ultimately Normandy.

The Friends of Christchurch Station, a small group of volunteers, was set up in 2007. Thanks to them, the station is adorned with colourful seasonal planting and has been able to offer refreshments. Councillor Fred Neale is one of the volunteers.

'Everything we do is geared towards raising funds for planting. Ultimately we'd like to see the refreshment room on Platform 1 for London-bound passengers, with the current room on Platform 2 used for exhibitions. Although we only have four or five active volunteers, we manage to get the refreshment room open most weekday mornings, which I know customers appreciate. Whatever people ask for, we've tried to provide. We care about the station and passengers and see other things that need tending. The station was looking quite dilapidated when we started, but one thing led to another, including replacement of broken bricks and encouraging the train operator to repaint the station. We all feel we're doing a valuable job for tourism in Christchurch.'

Margaret Pitcher is a volunteer planter.

'I love flowers and gardening and I like the station to look nice. We have two intense periods of activity each year when we renew planting, and summer can be busy with watering two to three times a week if it's hot. We receive compliments from so many people, telling us the station looks "so lovely"; that makes all the effort worthwhile.'

Christchurch Hospital

The hospital is located about half-a-mile from the railway station on Fairmile Road. The building was originally Christchurch's second workhouse, established in 1881 after the original (now Red House Museum) had become inadequate. Many workhouse buildings still survive, although 'H Block', the old workhouse infirmary, has been lost as the hospital site is redeveloped to

Christchurch Hospital – from workhouse to NHS hospital.

provide a new nursing home and assisted-living accommodation.

From 1896 children were housed in Cottage Homes, constructed the other side of Fairmile, arranged around a central green, the last home being demolished in 1966. There is a story that residents of a house in Emily Close heard children's voices in an empty upstairs bedroom; the house is on the site of Cottage Home No. 5. The Cottage Homes girl-guide troop was invited to Highcliffe Castle in 1928 to meet Queen Mary (the consort of George V) for what was a rare treat, as the workhouse regime was almost unremittingly harsh.

One of the wards during the Great War, with nurses and wounded soldiers. Rose Selfridge and daughters Rosalie and Violette joined the Red Cross and worked initially at the hospital. (© Hampshire County Council. Provided by Hampshire Cultural Trust.)

Castles Home Hardware

Castles Home Hardware (known locally simply as Castles) has been an independent business in Bargates since the early 1920s. Joseph Castle started the business in Pokesdown around 1908, before setting up the Christchurch shop in 1922 for son Leonard. The current owner is Roger Mason.

'My father was an indentured apprentice at Pokesdown around 1928/29, serving a 5-year apprenticeship before coming to work for Leonard Castle in 1937. With Leonard having no children, it was my Dad who bought the business from him

in 1969 when he retired, having managed it for many years on his behalf. Dad retained the original name of Castles though as it's so well known. Hardware stores are often known by their original names, even when they change ownership. I joined Dad in 1970 and became sole owner when he passed away, aged 96. He still helped out a couple of mornings a week even in his 90s.'

When asked about the famous *Two Ronnies* sketch set in a hardware store and how often they get asked for fork handles (four candles), Roger says:

Castles' catchphrase since the 1970s has been 'We have everything (almost!)'.

'We get people coming in quite regularly trying that one on us. It's nice really that people think of us that way. We used to get more practical jokes when there were more apprentices around. Being a bit wet behind the ear, they were sent in for items like elbow grease, a skirting board ladder and a long weight for a chimney. One chap tried to pull a fast one on his wife, asking her to come in for a new bubble for his spirit level. We had a choice of three! Customers say it's nice to come into a proper shop with a real smell. We have loyal customers, with people coming from 20 miles away. We've even had people who used to live here returning on holiday and bringing a list with them! We feel we've found our niche market. When big DIY chains opened we adapted and adjusted our stock to suit. This kept us distinctive. One thing we're famed for is selling things individually, for example a T-hinge for a shed door. At Castles we'll sell you one if that's all you need. We have a good team. They have practical common sense and do DIY at home. Oh and we only wear warehouse coats (à la Two Ronnies) when we're doing something dirty!'

Stewarts Garden Centre

Stewarts, just off Somerford roundabout, was the first purpose-built garden centre in the UK. It was opened in October 1961 by TV personality Percy Thrower. However, the business dates back much further, to Charles Stewart, an 18th-century Scottish plantsman, who was growing forestry trees as early as 1742; thus 'Stewarts' has been a family business for centuries. It extended to a seed business and nursery/plant houses open to the public, before coming to Dorset in 1859, when David Stewart (the grandson of Charles) opened a nursery in Ferndown. There is a second garden centre at Broomhill, Holt, near Wimborne, which replaced the Ferndown operation in the 1950s.

Exploring

Stanpit Marsh, a quiet nature area.

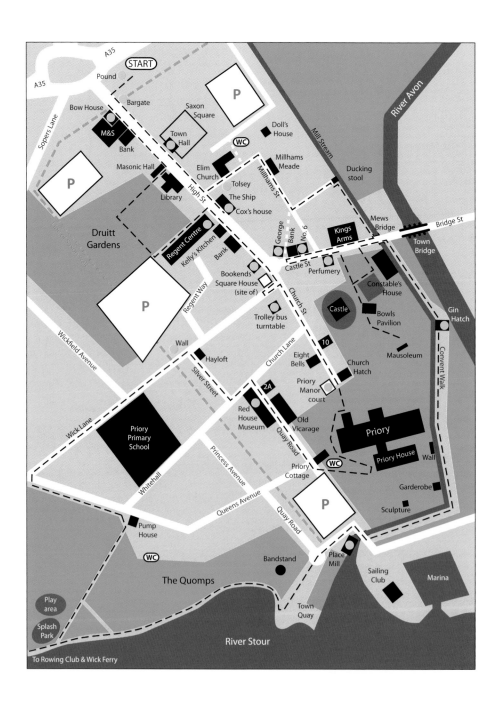

Walk 1: Historic Town Centre and Blue Plaques

Start: Pound Lane (top of High Street, close to subway under Fountain Way)
Finish: Top of High Street, west side
Approx. distance: 3 km

A plaque above the **Pound Lane** sign recalls that stray animals were once kept in a fenced enclosure here (the pound). The Hayward was the court official appointed to the task of rounding them up.

Turn into the High Street and walk towards the Priory. There is a plaque telling how a **bargate** stood here from around the 12th to the mid-18th century. The town would have been secure behind its wall, with the gate closed each night.

Town Hall. (Courtesy of Allan Wood.)

Saxon Square is fronted by the old 1746 **Town Hall**, which once stood at the junction of High Street and Castle Street in the middle of the 'square', before moving to its current location in Saxon Square in 1860. There was a lecture hall to the rear, hosting entertainments in Victorian times, and hustings to the front, when general elections were rowdy affairs with no secret ballot. The shopping precinct was built on the site of a Saxon burial ground.

Cross Millhams Street. **The Ship** has been a drinking place since the late 17th century. A former landlord, a German immigrant (*c.* 1895), was called Mr Booz!

Next-door is **Superdrug** – the plaque in its entrance tells how the house of Robert Harvey Cox stood here. Cox introduced fusee chain manufacturing to Christchurch in 1790 and his

workshop was to the rear. The house and workshop were pulled down in 1965.

Go back past the pub, turning right into Millhams Street. Another plaque here on the right describes how Christchurch's original town hall stood here (**Old Tolsey**), first mentioned by deed in 1572 and demolished in 1788. This was superseded by the current Town Hall, as mentioned.

Across the road is **Christchurch Christian Centre**, formerly a United Reformed Church and now an Elim Pentecostal Church. 'Dissenters' (people separate from the Church of England) have worshipped here for centuries. Built in 1867, the building has a fine spire and in 1872 the trustees boasted it was warmed by 'heating apparatus'.

To the east of the church was a scout-hut and schoolroom (now 'The Cloisters' housing development). Only the schoolmistress's small cottage remains in the corner, nicknamed the **Doll's House**.

Turn right into the continuation of Millhams Street. **Millhams Meade** is a fine row of 18th-century houses, once home to prominent solicitor Richard Sharp, named in the 1841 census.

Take a left into Ducking Stool Lane. At the end is a replica **ducking stool**, supposedly used to punish 'scolds' (women found guilty of verbal abuse, brawling or other antisocial behaviour) by dipping them in the Mill Stream. The original stool dated to the mid-14th century and there is an interpretation panel. The half-mile-long Mill Stream was most likely constructed by monks about 1,200 years ago to turn the wheel at Place Mill. Opposite the ducking stool used to be Town Mill.

With your back to the Mill Stream, turn immediately left along the raised Ducking Stool Walk and continue downstream to **Mews Bridge**. Turn right along Castle Street, passing the **Kings Arms**. Built in 1803 as Humby's (hotel) on the site of a 17th-century inn, it was the venue for fashionable balls when the wealthy visited the 'watering place' of Georgian Mudeford. In 1965 the Australian music group The Seekers performed here at Gardner's Christmas party (Gardner's was an electronics firm with a factory in Somerford Road).

Don't miss the blue plaque on the wall of No. 6/6a, a 17th-century mercer's house and home to the **Ferrey family**. George Ferrey was the Priory organist for 50 years and brother Benjamin an eminent ecclesiastical architect, who designed, among other things, Bournemouth's first hotel, the Royal Bath, in 1838 and the Corn Exchange in Dorchester.

Next-door, **Lloyds Bank** was once the White Hart (1685) and then a Masonic Lodge (1750), frequented by Lt Alex Mount RN, who sailed with Captain Cook.

Beyond is **Ye Olde George Inn**, Christchurch's oldest surviving pub (earliest reference to it is in 1652), which once looked out on the town's market square, with Square House opposite. Intrepid smuggler John Streeter used Royal Mail coaches stopping here to distribute contraband around the country. Smugglers' tunnels once led to the Quay and castle. Inside the courtyard was a barred window (now bricked up) where prisoners waited for the Emerald Coach to take them to Poole and deportation to Australia. Have a peek inside the courtyard (right) and you'll see a representation of a prisoner. The narrow passageway next to the pub once led to Town Mill.

The building next door to the left used to be the **Creamery Tea Rooms**, ideally placed just down from the tram terminus. Looking across the road at the corner house (**No. 1 Church Street**), above the doorway the large blank painted area would have been used for advertising in the past.

Cross Castle Street at the crossing and walk back down Castle Street towards the river. You come to the **New Forest Perfumery**, parts of which are 13th century. It is sometimes mistaken for the old court house (demolished in 1888), which was next-door over the castle gateway, and there is a small lock-up in the courtyard. The Perfumery building did nevertheless have a court function (with the court leet) until 1920, as officials were elected in the back room, including the Hayward (who looked after the pound and was town crier) and oddities such as the inspector of chimneys, ale taster (nice

work if you can get it) and bread weigher. Once a butchers, meat hooks are visible above the window and inside in ceiling beams of the back room. In its butchery days locals nicknamed it Dirty Gert's as the owner was not overly fastidious about hygiene. There is also a tale of a smuggling tunnel running under the building to the Quay. In the 1870s it was a shoemakers, then a bookshop, before in 1944 becoming a perfumery, where the mixing of perfumes was carried out, until in 1996 it became a tea room.

Take an immediate right after the Perfumery and walk through where the court house was. Proceed past the replica stocks and whipping post to **Christchurch Castle** motte, erected by the Normans in the 12th century to dominate the town.

Walk through the arch ahead to see a large ornate wall, the remains of a **mausoleum** constructed for a wealthy local woman, Mrs Perkins (d. 1783), who allegedly had a fear of being buried alive. She asked to be placed near the school so the boys would hear if she revived; also that her coffin lid be left unsecured and to ensure the mausoleum could be opened from inside. She was later removed from here to be reburied

with her husband Lt-Gen J.F. Perkins (d. 1803) in the family vault in Winkton.

In front of the mausoleum is a **rose garden**, planted in 2014, and a **memorial** commemorating the centenary of the outbreak of WW1, which saw Christchurch lose more than 120 people. You can go past the mausoleum, following the Mill Stream behind the Priory to Town Quay, but our walk heads back past the castle to Castle Street.

Back-track to the former bowls pavilion and green occupying the castle bailey. There is a plaque in the pavement at the rear of the small car park (inside the entrance gate to the bowling green) noting that this was once a tea garden.

The large ruin on the green is that of **Constable's House**, built *c.* 1160 by Baldwin de Redvers, accommodating the Lord of the Manor's constable or bailiff in greater luxury than the castle keep allowed. Note the Norman chimney, one of only five in the country, water gate and privy, which extends across the Mill Stream.

Next is the River Avon and **Town Bridge**, a medieval five-arched bridge. Cannonballs were retrieved from under the bridge, leftovers from the Civil War. Admire the views upstream and downstream. Sometimes there are fisher-

men in the large tethered punt here.

Take the path just before the bridge (**Convent Walk**), continuing between the river and Mill Stream. Ferries once used to call here, but no more. The doorway through the east wall of Constable's House (where the railings are) gave access from the Mill Stream to the castle storeroom.

Convent Walk was laid in 1911 to mark the coronation of George V, with a brief ceremony at the arched doorway part-way along known as the **Gin Door** (or Hatch); a sapling was also planted opposite and is now a fully grown **Coronation Oak**. The Hatch was used by the miller at Place Mill to control the stream when in flood (excess water being returned to the Avon via a short sluice). Flat-

bottomed punts entered the Mill Steam here, accessing the water-gate of Constable's House. The area below the Priory was once called the 'Werkes', where stone was landed for building the church and castle.

On the opposite side of the Mill Stream, the **stone wall** a short distance downstream may be the remains of the Priory kitchen. Before the path turns right you also pass opposite the site of the monastic **garderobe** (privy) which jutted over the stream.

The end of Convent Walk brings you to ancient **Place Mill Bridge** and **Place Mill**. The mill was mentioned in *Domesday* and was still working in 1908, before being used as a boat house. There is a tale suggesting the miller concealed smuggled contraband in the deep grain hoppers at the top of the building.

Place Mill. (Courtesy of Allan Wood.)

Walk ahead, arriving at **Town Quay**, once an industrial quay but now a ferry-stop, boat-hire centre and pleasant riverside walk.

Follow the path alongside the Stour, past the playground, splash-park, public slipway, Sea Cadets and Rowing Club, until you reach the **Captain's Club Hotel**. This modern building occupies part of the site of former Pontins

holiday camp. Here also is Wick Ferry, which can be used to cross to the Bournemouth side and Tuckton Tea Gardens.

Retrace your steps to **Mayors Mead** (now a car park), which once had a miniature railway running around it, with its station close to the current playground. Past the splash-park turn left and take the footpath across the **Quomps** to Queens Avenue. On the right here is the **Pump House**, a former pumping station (now offices), as the land used to flood here.

There are flood gates in the wall at the rear of the Quomps, including ones by the public conveniences.

Turn left, then right into Wick Lane. Pass **Priory Primary School**, which has been sited here since 1867. The school began life in 1662 inside the Priory in St Michael's Loft, and there was a brief spell in cramped conditions in the High Street (1829–67) until it moved to its current premises.

Just before Wick Lane car park, a plaque on the left on the white building recalls that **Saxon defences** were aligned here, heading in both directions. On the corner of Wick Lane and Silver Street is the **Hayloft Gallery**, a former coach house and stables. Note how the corner brickwork is curved so that wheels of passing carts didn't 'hook' the building and cause damage.

Go down Silver Street on the right, then turn left and right into Quay Road. On the left is No. 2a **The Old Brewhouse**, which as the name suggests used to be a brewery (though it is difficult to see this today).

The building that is now **Red House Museum** was formerly a barn, and then became the workhouse (1764–1885). Herbert Druitt determinedly preserved and recorded every aspect of the town's past and his collection eventually formed the core of the museum, which he gifted to the town. The museum opened in 1951, 8 years after his death.

Continue along the road past the **old vicarage** on your left. Walk beyond the Priory, past **Priory Cottage** (fomerly a porter's lodge), which along with the church survived the Dissolution, and into the car park. Turn left to see **Priory House** (*c.* 1776, now a gift shop, café, etc.), built on the site of the Priory's monastic buildings; note the crumbling remains on the Priory's south wall.

Enter the **Priory** by the north porch to explore this impressive building. The walk continues from this porch, heading towards town along what was once an elm **avenue**, following in the footsteps of Royal visitors Kaiser Wilhelm II (1907) and Queen Elizabeth II (1966).

At the **gates** turn around for a last look at the Priory and note the unfinished parapet to the left (east end), work abandoned at the Dissolution. The upper storey (east end) is St Michael's Loft, once home to the town school and

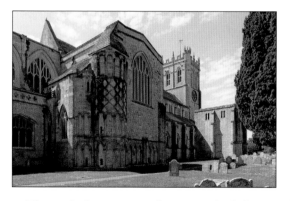

now a museum. The area between the north transept and north porch was an archery ground in medieval times and may have acted as a school playground. You may hear the sound of the Priory's seven bells – two were hung in 1370, among the oldest still rung regularly in the country.

Through the gate is a plaque on the left recording that a **medieval court** for Priory Manor stood here until the 19th century. The site is now occupied by the new **Vicarage. Church Street**, which takes you from the Priory to the former market square, used to be known as Meringue Alley because of the proliferation of tea shops.

On the right is **Church Hatch**, a splendid early-18th-century house, once home to Major-General Sir Owen Tudor Burne (1903–9, a veteran of the Crimean War and Indian Mutiny), Mrs Perkins (mentioned earlier) and publisher Walter Hutchinson (1930s), who installed the first direct phone line between Christchurch and his London HQ.

Ye Olde Eight Bells Shoppe, formerly a pub called the Eight Bells until 1907, is named after the seven bells of the Priory (a bit like golf's 19th hole). A one-time smuggler's haunt, it is alleged there is a tunnel from here to the Ship in Distress at Stanpit. The building bears the date 1450.

On the other side of the street is **No. 10**. This once belonged to the medieval charity **Hospital of Mary Magdalen** which had buildings at the Magdalen Lane corner of Barrack Road Recreation Ground (outside the town walls) for the treatment of leprosy. The first endowment of the leper hospital occurred in 1317 and the first master was Richard Wade. Returning Crusaders with skin and other infectious diseases were housed here. Mary Magdalen was the female disciple Jesus cured of 'infirmities'. The charity (Hospital of St Mary Magdalen at Christchurch) still exists to help the needy and must be one of the oldest continuously operating in the country. No. 10 became a house in the mid-19th century and in the 1920s was a dining room (café) owned by the gloriously named Elsie Titt. The old hospital site now has a block of flats on it.

When you reach the former market square at the junction of High Street and Castle Street turn left into **Wick Lane**. On the left is a plaque recording that a **trolley bus turntable** stood here (under the arch). This was the

end of the line from Bournemouth and buses were turned here until 1969.

The turntable, believed to be the last in the country, can just be seen through the gates in what was once the yard of the Dolphin Hotel.

A bedecked trolley bus parked outside the Dolphin Hotel in Church Street on 8 April 1936, the day the service started. (© Hampshire County Council. Provided by Hampshire Cultural Trust.)

The Square House and High Street,Christchurch, Hampshire, by Benjamin Ferrey. (From the Christchurch Historical Society Portfolio Vol. 1 1920 by kind permission of the Christchurch History Society to whom all enquiries should be made.)

Return to the former market square and walk up the High Street. On the left where the arcade is there used to be an elegant 18th-century mansion, **Square House** (now demolished). It was built by a local brewer *c.* 1776, with features believed to be the work of the famous Adam brothers, and named after its position overlooking the market square. A Dr Hartford is known to have lived here around 1912, but it was sadly demolished in 1958.

Beyond the arcade, the house now **Bookends** was given in trust by John Clingan in 1714 to benefit the poor, and the Clingan's Trust, which still exists, funded apprenticeships in various occupations. It has helped some 3,000 young people and continues to provide grants to local students aged under 25. After Clingan, the house was the premises of drapers Ferrey and Sons (1816–1936), with Benjamin Ferrey, the famous architect, living here as a child. It was Smiths furniture showroom before Bookends, which still pays rent to the Clingan Trust for the building.

NatWest Bank is housed in a fine Victorian mansion built by James Kemp Welch (1806–87), an eminent surgeon, deacon, lighting inspector and four-times mayor of Christchurch. When the Christchurch and Wimborne Bank took over the building (1823–41) it printed its own bank notes (£1, £5 and £10) there.

Kelly's Kitchen occupies No. 55, the former Jarvis Radio shop (of 67 years), the building dating to 1843. It has interesting carvings around the windows. The first display of a TV in the High Street occurred here in 1952.

The Art Deco **Regent Centre** started life as a bookshop (Caxton House Bookshop) and then became a cinema in 1931 and a bingo hall, then cinema again. It still hosts cinema, theatre, opera, concerts and dance productions, as well as art exhibitions in the lower foyer.

Turn left down the alley just after the Regent Centre into **Druitt Gardens**, formerly the garden of the Druitt family home which was bequeathed to the town. Explore and enjoy the Gardens and wood sculptures here.

Leave the Gardens past Druitt Hall and the U3A and return to the High Street. The **library** building dates to 1844, when it was built for solicitor James Druitt as a residence; he later gave it to the town. James' son Herbert accumulated an enormous local history archive, now in possession of the Christchurch History Society.

On the left, somewhat obscured by bus shelters, is the 1837 **Masonic Hall**. Note the ornamental urn on the roof and its grand doorway. Between the Library and Hall was once the national school (1829–67, mentioned earlier); such schools were run by the Church of England in the 19th century for children of the poor.

The 1800s saw much change in the **High Street**, with paved sidewalks (1835), the first purpose-built shops (1844), gas lighting (1850) and street numbering (1894). In 1832, 1,500 men enjoyed a beef and plum pudding dinner in the High Street to celebrate the passing of the Great Reform Bill (the first great parliamentary reform bill, which included an extension of the male franchise; women were not permitted to vote until 1918). Approaching the top of the street you are back in the vicinity of the former bargate and Saxon wall. Midland Bank (now **HSBC**) once had Mr

Selfridge as an account holder. The bank manager of the time honoured his prestigious customer by having the pillars and imposing façade installed in 1920. The **M&S site** next-door was once a garage (1951–74).

Cellars and tunnels were reputedly accessible from **Bow House** (the next building along), a throwback to smuggling days. Bow House (a brewer's house,

see wall plaque here) is all that remains of Christchurch Brewery, an extensive brewery complex established in 1723. The house became Hart's Museum in the early 20th century, displaying stuffed birds and animals. The rest of the brewery was demolished by the 1970s to make way for a car park behind M&S.

Walk 2: Stanpit and Purewell

Start and finish: Two Riversmeet Leisure Centre
Approx. distance: 5 km

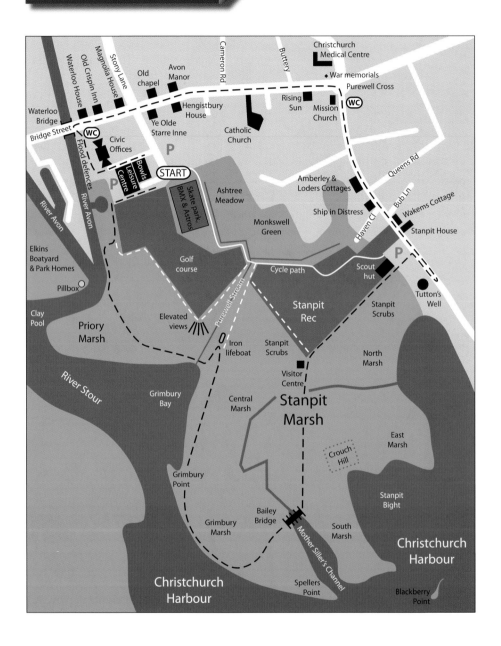

(Even on dry days on Stanpit Marsh, Wellington boots may be needed. With spring tides the area may flood; check tide tables. A Dog Control Order is in place and wardens patrol the area: dogs must be on leads to protect nesting birds, though they can be off-lead on the small stretch of shingle beach, but only along the shoreline and in the water. Keep to the main path, except on Crouch Hill, a viewpoint for birdwatchers.)

Take the path from the Leisure Centre entrance, following signs for 'Stanpit via Priory View Footpath'. Bear left at the gate and along the path, heading over the stile on the right, which brings you out facing the River Avon. (*Note: if the marsh is particularly wet, you may instead take the cycleway/footpath around the golf course (see map) and rejoin the walk at the iron lifeboat or the Visitor Centre.*)

Continue along the river bank for views of the Priory, Hengistbury Head, Elkins Boatyard and the river, which flows either side of an island.

Walk to the bend, where the footpath continues across the first of several **railway-sleeper paths** over the marsh. Across the river is a **pillbox**, a relic of WW2; here the two branches of the River Avon rejoin. Just further on, the Stour comes in from the left, the two rivers then heading into Christchurch Harbour.

The path takes you towards **Grimbury Bay** and over stiles at Purewell Stream. Detour left for a short distance to a fenced-off iron **lifeboat**, which formerly served a Liberty ship (one of the US cargo ships built during WW2). After the war the lifeboat was used locally, until the early 1950s when a storm washed her here, the boat being then stripped and abandoned and she now seems to be returning to nature.

Retrace your steps and head towards **Grimbury Point**. Reaching the shingle beach, walk along until the path turns inland (at the seat) to the **Bailey Bridge**. This is a WW2 prototype of the famous bridge. It crosses **Mother Siller's Channel**, which around the end of the 18th century was used for conveying large amounts of contraband. From here you can see the harbour entrance, Mudeford Quay and the Sandbank with its colourful beach huts.

Walk over Bailey Bridge, noting the view across to fenced-off **Crouch Hill**, the highest point on the marsh (5 m above sea level), which once had a

barrow on top with Bronze Age material. The fencing is to reduce erosion by livestock and visitors. The Bronze Age artefacts, including a well-preserved cremation urn, can be seen in Red House Museum.

Continue to **Stanpit Marsh Visitor Centre**. The centre is volunteer run, with assistance of the Countryside Service, and is well worth a visit. They offer evening walks, have visits from schools and other youth groups, organise wildlife hunts, competitions, and provide identification charts and maps. You can also look at the archives and Christchurch Harbour Ornithological Group records. The list of recent wildlife sightings is impressive. Children are well catered for, with a touch-and-feel area, colouring and child-friendly information.

Carry on along the footpath, passing the **Recreation Ground**, reclaimed in the 1960s, previously an extension of the marsh. Go round the side of the **sea scout hut**. The hut is named *TS Orestes* after *HMS Orestes*, the Revenue cutter that took part in the Battle of Mudeford (1784).

Emerging onto Stanpit road (literally 'stony pit'), turn right to **Tutton's Well**, an ancient, never-ending water supply 'of uncommon purety' renowned for its medicinal qualities and promoted as 'Christchurch Elixir'. The name could date to a George Touting who it is said knew of the spring in the mid-17th century. The well was capped in 1941. The surrounding green was used by fishermen to dry nets and by smugglers landing contraband.

Back-track along the road, past the rec. Look out for the end-on house across the road, **Stanpit House**, probably a yeoman farmer's abode dating to the mid-18th century, and, beyond it, **Wakems Cottage**, also 18th century. Note the blocked-up windows. From 1696 Window Tax was levied on people according to wealth, and generally the more windows you had, the larger the house you owned. The tax wasn't repealed until 1851.

Walk beyond **Bub Lane**, named after Walter Bub, an 18th-century seafarer, to the **Ship in Distress**. Former landlady Hanna Siller married the landlord of the Haven Inn at the time of the Battle of Mudeford. After he died, she moved to the Ship where she became 'protecting angel' of smugglers. In the 18th and 19th centuries

Mother Siller's Channel was navigable by small boats up to the inn, making this an ideal place for storing contraband.

Just beyond the pub are remains of the former **Avon Brewery** (a pair of semi-detached cottages called 'Amberley' and 'Loders'). Before becoming a brewery, infamous John Streeter once conducted 'business' here. Tobacco racketeer and smuggler, Streeter was involved in the Battle of Mudeford and was adept at sneaking in casks of liquor hidden in grain cargo. His snuff factory (using smuggled tobacco) later became a boys' school (1841), and then was redeveloped as a brewery in the 1890s.

Continue to **Purewell Cross**, the scene of a shooting in 1643 in the early

stages of the Civil War. Sentry John Swithin was on watch when approached by John Sope, who ignored four or five orders to 'stand', whereupon Swithin shot and killed him. Swithin was released, having only done his duty.

On the corner is the **Mission Church of St John** (1880), built for Purewell/Stanpit folk who couldn't make it to the Priory.

Turn left into Purewell. Across the road is the **war memorial**, with several plaques, including one to US 405th fighter group which operated from

Christchurch Airfield (Somerford) in WW2. The famous epitaph 'When you go home, tell them of us and say, for your tomorrow, we gave our today' by John Maxwell Edmonds was inspired by an epigram for the fallen at the Battle of Thermopylae, Greece, 480 BC.

Behind is **Christchurch Medical Centre** (*c.* 1970), occupying the site of former Purewell Farm and some of its buildings.

Just down the road, the **Rising Sun** dates to the late 18th century and is now a Thai restaurant. Continue past roads Buttery (right) and Fernlea (left) to the **Catholic Church of the Immaculate Conception and St Joseph** (*c.* 1866). There used to be a campanile (Italianate bell-tower) on the roof and also a Victorian presbytery (priest's house) at right-angles to the rear left of the church.

Carry on past Cameron Road and Marsh Lane. The large house on the left, **Hengistbury House**, dates to the 1830s and was built by Samuel Bayly who owned a drapery business in Castle Street. He sold the house to Rev Joseph Fletcher in 1859, after which it

opened as a boys' school, which closed in 1868 after eight pupils tragically drowned at Mudeford.

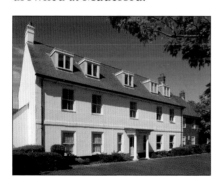

Opposite is **Avon Manor** (previously Amsterdam House), its former name suggesting Dutch connections. In 1579, when John Hastings introduced the manufacture of serge cloth from Holland, he brought over Dutch weavers, who may have been installed in an earlier house here, or it may refer to the Dutch dredging experts employed to improve navigation in the harbour.

The building has been a school, lamp works, hotel and aircraft repair works, and was occupied by a surgeon and even a gypsy who pedaled 'Romany remedies'.

Continue past Tamlyn's Farm Mews. Across the road is **Chapel Studios**, previously a Wesleyan chapel built in 1834 and rebuilt in 1890.

At the crossroads, another pub, **Ye Olde Starre Inne**, was a beer-house as long ago as 1844, when Henry Button was the publican, although it has been occupied in the past by a tailor, corn-factor (person dealing in corn) and baker.

Back at Stony Lane, rather than turning left for the Leisure Centre, continue straight on into Bridge Street. On the right is **Magnolia House**, now a veterinary clinic. Old Magnolia House (demolished in 1970) had been home to 19th-century surgeons and a veterinary surgeon in the 1930s. Christchurch Interiors was formerly an inn, **Crispin Inn** (1802–1920).

Ahead is **Waterloo Bridge**, built in 1816–17 and named after the Battle of

Waterloo. There are pleasant views of the river from here. The imposing pink building on the right with a fine coach arch is **Waterloo House**, built in 1886 and owned by George Pope, who ran one of Christchurch's original 'motor garages' from here.

Note the **flood gate, stone and plaque** to the side of the bridge. These record the opening of the Lower Avon

flood defence scheme in 1998 by Baroness Maddock (formerly Diana Maddock MP), who won a famous Christchurch by-election for the Liberal Democrats 5 years earlier, with one of the largest swings ever recorded.

Continue along the right-hand side of the **Civic Offices**, opened by Prince and Princess Michael of Kent in 1980, through more **flood gates**. Flood defences were vital as Purewell is only 1.8 m above sea-level and there has been frequent flooding in the past.

When you reach the rear of the offices, turn left for the Leisure Centre, past the Bowls Club.

Walk 3: St Catherine's Hill

Start and finish: Small car park at foot of St Catherine's Hill Lane off Fairmile Road
Approx. distance: 5 km

(Note: adders live on St Catherine's Hill, so walkers should keep to paths and stout footwear is recommended. Please take heed of any signs, as some paths are seasonal.)

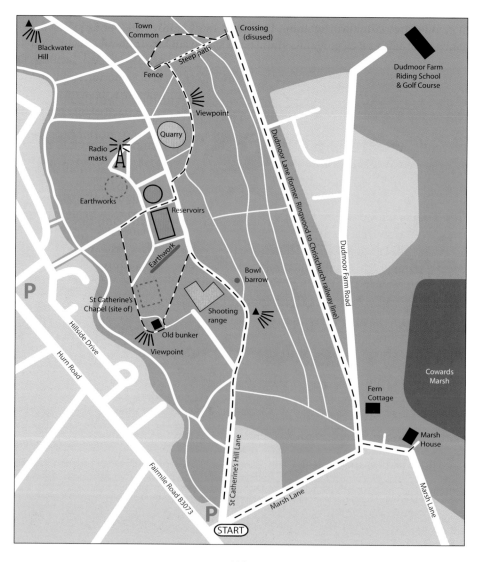

Walk up the gravel track (St Catherine's Hill Lane), which starts close to a sign to Dudmoor Farm. After some houses, at the five-bar gate, go straight on, past the information board.

To the left is a track for **Christchurch Gun Club**; if the red flag is flying, shooting is taking place and you will hear loud bangs. The Royal Horse Artillery, based at Christchurch Barracks, used to train horses and drivers on the Hill in 1815, the year of the Battle of Waterloo, and the Dragoons in 1851, although the poor state of the approach road discouraged this. Troops also practised on the Hill during both World Wars.

The path bends slightly to the right, and then comes to a fence. Bear right to an **OS trig-point and orientation stone**, the latter erected in 2014. On a clear day you can see the Needles on the Isle of Wight, the Priory and Hengistbury Head behind, and admire the sweep of the River Avon. The Hill rises 50 m above sea level, Christchurch's highest point, and has probably been used as a look-out and beacon since prehistoric times.

Being a discrete distance from the town, the Hill became a favoured place for quarantine and it appears there was a pest-house here from the mid-18th century for contagious cases. There may also be plague pits, as Christchurch enforced quarantine *c.* 1665 when bubonic plague was a risk. A watch was maintained, with anyone arriving from London not admitted to the town for 20 days. The threat was so serious one watchman who neglected his duties was placed in the stocks for 4 hours, the last recorded occasion the town's stocks were used. The Black Death also visited the town in 1350, causing many deaths.

Continue up the hill, and as the path forks bear left. You will see a **bowl barrow** on the right through trees. This is an ancient burial mound. Another barrow on the Hill contained cremated remains dating from about 1400 BC. Eight of these barrows or tumuli, largely thought to be

Bronze Age, are scattered across the hill. There is also a banked earthwork just to the south of the radio masts, thought to date from the Iron Age.

Less than 6000 ha of **Dorset heathland** remains, and this area is a fine example of this type of habitat, of national importance because of the wildlife it supports. Birch and pine have to be controlled, otherwise such valuable heathland reverts to scrub woodland.

Take the next small path on the left, back around and above the shooting range, which brings you out by some concrete remains. After the war, a **Royal Observer Corps atom-bomb reporting station** was constructed under the Hill. Its purpose was to detect and report any atom-bomb attacks during the Cold War. A three-man volunteer team would have occupied the post for up to 3 weeks, reporting the location of any flash or explosion as well as the prevailing wind direction so that any fallout plumes could be predicted. The post is long closed and overgrown.

Skirt round the concrete to enjoy the viewpoint. Then continue along the ridge-top path, bending to the right with houses below to your left.

You come to a lone tree in the middle of a junction of paths. On the right there is an earth bank, part of the earthworks that led to and surrounded old **St Catherine's Chapel** here. No foundations have been found so it is likely the stone was removed and reused elsewhere, perhaps on the Priory. Local legend has it that the Priory could have been built on the Hill, but attempts to build were thwarted by stones mysteriously 'walking' down to the current Priory site, where presumably some greater-being had decided the new church should be. A chapel existed on the Hill until the Dissolution in 1539. Excavations in the late 1960s found evidence of a series of chapels constructed between the 11th and 16th centuries and a fragment of limestone decorated with the Christian symbol of a fish. Hills were often dedicated to St Catherine, who according to legend was executed for her faith and buried on the summit of Mount Sinai.

The site may have been a **Roman signal station** (Roman pottery has been found around here), and it was certainly used as a **beacon** from medieval times until the Napoleonic Wars, to be lit when invasion threatened. Sometimes the Hill was on the receiving end. A German bomber dropped incendiaries during WW2, one of several air-raids on the town, and the Hill smoldered for some days. The Hill still suffers from the occasional but extensive heath fire.

Keeping the lone tree on your right, continue on, heading towards the radio masts. An original base station and 30-m-high tower form part of a mobile phone network, covering the Poole–Southampton–Fordingbridge area as well as coastal shipping.

At the oak tree, turn right towards the **reservoirs**. These contain water drawn from the Avon, treated at Knapp Mill, then pumped up the Hill. From the reservoirs the water flows under gravity to supply Christchurch, east Bournemouth and the hospital at Littledown. (Incidentally, the Hill used to be called 'Richedoun' (meaning 'great hill'), distinguishing it from 'Lytildoun' ('little hill'), now Littledown.) Each reservoir holds 9.1 million litres (2 million gallons) of treated water.

The waterworks opened in 1895 and included the purchase, from the Earl of Malmesbury at a cost of £200, of 0.8 ha for the first reservoir. The second reservoir was added in 1963.

Walk between the reservoirs to the path ahead, turning left. Buddleia, brambles and gorse here attract butterflies and other insects. After about 75 m there are two paths on the right, either side of a wooden bridleway sign. Take either, descending to the **quarry**. This was dug in the 19th century to extract sand and gravel and has exposed layers of geology. Between 35 and 45 million years ago the Hill formed part of a river delta with a subtropical climate, similar to today's Nile. There is orange sand and clay at the top, laid down a million years or so ago; lower layers are older.

Walk up to the fence line and turn left along the ridge. Note the **view of the Avon valley**. The brown building in the near distance with a white building to the right (with solar roof panels) is Dudmoor Farm, where there is a golf course and riding stables. The old, straight railway line can be clearly seen.

Continue along this ridge path following the fence. You pass **two seats** with plaques stating that the nature reserve (Town Common Nature Reserve which borders the Hill) is dedicated to local musician and herpetologist Donald Street (1940–81), the author of *Reptiles of Central and Northern Europe*.

The path bends left, still following the fence. At the end of the fence, turn right. At the bottom of the dip, bear right down a rough track onto the open heathland below. This is Town Common and the path brings you out at a crossing of the old Ringwood to Christchurch **railway line**, which closed to passengers in 1935. If you turned left here you would come to the Avon Causeway pub, formerly Hurn Station on the way to Ringwood. Instead turn right for Christchurch along what is now called Dudmoor Lane.

At the end of the track where it meets the tarmac road, straight ahead is **Fern Cottage**. This used to be a level-crossing keeper's house.

Turn right into Dudmoor Farm Road, leading into Marsh Lane, where there was an isolation hospital, although nothing remains of this. Take a detour left onto a rough road, with some houses on the right; the second turn left brings you to **Marsh House**, the herdsman's house (*c.* 1750) and **Cowards Marsh**. This is ancient common land, documented to at least 1718, where animals can be grazed depending on the time of year.

Return to Dudmoor Farm Road. Turn left and continue back to the car park and main road, along Marsh Lane.

Walk 4: Mudeford

Start and finish: Mudeford Quay
Approx. distance: 5.5 km

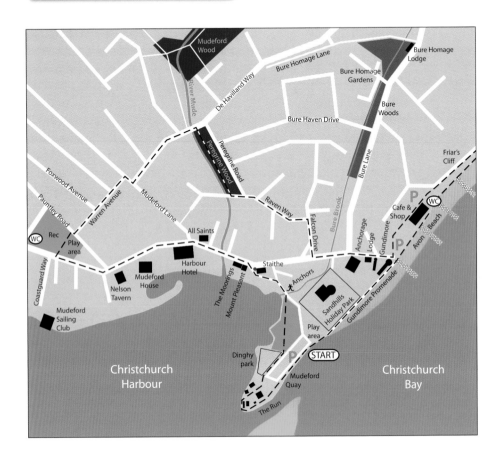

From the railings overlooking 'The Run' this stretch of quayside is a popular spot for crabbing. Walk towards the buildings on the Quay. The area is often busy with small boats entering and leaving Christchurch Harbour. Note the lobster pots stacked up on the quay.

Bear left past the Fish Stall and you'll probably see the flag flying for the Mudeford Ferry, taking passengers across to the Sandbank. You could take the ferry now or later and explore some of Hengistbury Head.

After the Fish Stall, the large buildings ahead of you are the original **Haven Inn** (left) and **Old Customs House** (right). During the Battle of Mudeford (1784) smugglers fired on customs men from the windows of the inn. W.

Allen, master of the sloop *HMS Orestes*, was shot dead and smuggler George Coombes was convicted of 'aiding and abetting', executed in London, then

hung in chains here. With smuggling increasing, more customs officers were recruited, some garrisoned in the Haven and adjacent cottages from 1823 to *c.* 1860, before moving to Stanpit. Note the **walls and flood gates** protecting the cottages here.

Continue past these to another row of cottages, some of which are holiday lets. Walk past these, bearing right along the harbour. There is a splendid view here. Bear right past the last cottage to see the lifeboat station and slipway of Mudeford **RNLI** and the clubhouse of **Highcliffe Sailing Club**.

Walk ahead past the dingy park, to the end of the car park, bearing left across the green. Just after crossing a small bridge over **Bure Brook** note the **anchors** (right), salvaged from Christchurch Bay and placed here in the 1970s. In this corner of the harbour a Roman ship was excavated in 1910.

Before the main road, turn left up Chichester Way, a one-way road. As you reach the junction with Mudeford road, note the Victorian **post box** (*c.* 1855) on the right, still in use, with an unusual vertical slot and flap. The design didn't catch on as the Post Office realised that a horizontal slot, recessed under an overhanging top, kept the rain out better. It is said there are only three such boxes still in use in the country.

The house immediately behind the phone box and shelter is called **The Staithe**, which means a landing stage for loading and unloading cargo boats. The house was possibly built in Charles II's reign. Lady Agnes Charlotte Douglas, second wife of Major General Sir Owen Tudor Burne, lived here from 1883 until 1889.

Opposite the post box across Chichester Way is **Mount Pleasant**, and to the right of that **The Moorings**, a large block of buildings built *c.* 1730. A window in The Moorings was etched by a diamond with Dutch names, probably men working on improvements to the harbour navigation. These buildings have been used as a place of lodging, post office and school. Note the picture window on the side of the garages.

Walk beyond The Moorings and cross over the **River Mude**, just before reaching Mude Gardens. There are views of the river heading into the harbour over the wall on the left.

You arrive at **Christchurch Harbour Hotel** (previously Avonmouth Hotel). Built in the late 18th century as 'Mudeford House', its owners included a French Royalist (Col. Joseph de la Tour), who owned the house until 1844. One of his tenants was Lt-Gen John Brian Keane, a Peninsular War veteran under Wellington. The building was converted to a hotel in the mid-1930s.

Opposite is **All Saints Church**, built *c.* 1869 by Mortimer Ricardo, one of the owners of Bure Homage, as a chapel of ease for the convenience of parishioners who couldn't make it to the parish church. For a while it doubled-up as the village school (until 1873), the bell on the right rung to ensure the children's timeliness. Cross the road to visit the church. Inside are rolls of honour from both World Wars and memorials to 2nd-Lt Anson Shirley Hamilton, who died at the Battle of the Ancre in November 1916 (the final British attack of the Somme), aged 22, and pilot Victor Sherring, who was killed in action in February 1943, aged 32. All these memorials are on the wall opposite as you enter.

Continue walking along, past the hotel, looking out for **Mudeford House** (left), just after Mude Cottage. This early 19th-century house belonged to the White-White family, one of whom was reputedly involved in the slave trade.

Notice the plaque to the right of the gateway dated 1789. This refers to the original Mudeford House (now Christchurch Harbour Hotel), just passed. When this was renamed 'The Avonmouth' (c. 1871) the name 'Mudeford House' was transferred to this property.

Further on is the **Nelson Tavern** (c. 1890). The inn replaced two cottages, home in the mid-19th century to Jane West (1798–71), a remarkable lady, who ran Avon Beach bathing machines and was described as 'conductor of the baths' at Mudeford, providing both 'hot baths at a short notice' and 'tea services'.

SEA-BATHING, CHRISTCHURCH, Hants.
NOTICE is hereby given, that a BATHING MACHINE, constructed by N. Ford, on an improved plan of safety and conveniency, is established on the sea beach, near this town, where its want has long been lamented by the neighbouring Gentry and Strangers, who, from the openness of the coast, the easy declivity of the beach, and the purity of the water here, have been led to expect, and may now certainly obtain every advantage of health or pleasure which a sea bath and sea air in their purest states can possibly afford. Many inhabitants have resolved to accommodate visitors with lodgings, and other conveniencies to facilitate their access to the sea side.
N.B. Several houses to be lett, and good accommodations at the Inns.

A 1788 advertisement in a newspaper for sea bathing at Mudeford. (© Hampshire County Council. Provided by Hampshire Cultural Trust.)

Beyond is the **recreation ground**, home of Mudeford Cricket Club. The rec was laid out in 1888 on land opposite the Coastguard Station (Coastguard Way on the left recalls this). This may well have been the location for the customs men after they were moved from Mudeford Quay in 1860, as the original coastguard (the 'Preventative Water Guard' of 1809) had a primary objective of preventing smuggling.

At the beginning of the rec, just after the bus shelter, turn right, taking the footpath across the rec, noting the **plaque** on the right recording that this land was given for the use of the children of Mudeford and Stanpit (in the late 1940s). The original name for the rec was 'Sandwaste', a place where locals came to get their sand.

Exiting the rec, take the road ahead (Warren Avenue). The first road on the left, **Foxwood Avenue**, was the scene of one of Christchurch's saddest accidents. A US P-47 'Thunderbolt' fighter-bomber crashed on take-off from Christchurch Airfield in June 1944, brought down another, bombs exploded, bungalows in the road were destroyed and 16 were left dead and 18 injured, including personnel from the US Army Air Force and Hampshire Fire Service, plus local civilians.

Continue up to the T-junction with Mudeford Lane. Cross, taking the road ahead, De Havilland Way, which recalls the aircraft factory (formerly Airspeed) that occupied land here.

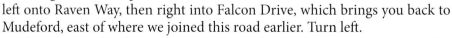

Further on, just past the De Havilland Way sign, cross the river and take the footpath through Peregrine Wood, running alongside the **River Mude**, which enters Christchurch Harbour at Smugglers Reach. Take this footpath, with the Mude on your right.

Carry straight on at the wooden footbridge, until the path runs out. Turn left onto Raven Way, then right into Falcon Drive, which brings you back to Mudeford, east of where we joined this road earlier. Turn left.

Almost immediately you come to **Sandhills Holiday Park** on your right, the house of that name built by Sir George Rose MP and visited by royalty (George III in 1789 and 1801 and possibly George IV in 1821). It is here where Mudeford's reputation as a 'watering-place' began. In order to reach his yacht, George III needed a temporary jetty of bathing machines; he also had a guard of honour and gun salute from the Scots Greys (Royal Cavalry Regiment).

Next on the right you pass **The Anchorage**, built in 1892 by George Hamilton Fletcher as a summer residence. He was the son and heir of one of the founders of the White Star Line and a close friend of Joseph Bruce

Ismay, the chairman and highest-ranking White Star official to survive *Titanic*. The house was sold to the Teachers' Provident Society *c.* 1935 as a convalescent home for retired teachers and now comprises retirement flats and maisonettes.

Carry on, past **Gundimore Lodge** (*c.* 1876), the entrance to the house Gundimore (which was designed to look like an Arab tent). It was built by Sir George Rose's son William Stuart Rose, a poet, artist and friend of the novelist Sir Walter Scott.

Just before the car park at Avon Beach, turn left onto a footpath which climbs the cliff behind the car park and beach. Walk ahead, with the beach and café below right and another, sunken car park on the left. Continue beyond the car park, admiring views of the Isle of Wight through the trees. Those with rougher bark are **Monterey Pines** from France, planted by Charles Stuart, owner of Bure Homage Estate; their root system has helped bind the cliff and prevent further erosion.

Further on, don't miss the **thatched cottage** flanked by somewhat futuristic houses. Drop down to promenade level, bearing right past beach huts, walking back towards **Avon Beach Café**. The shop is worth visiting, as it has a well-stocked book section.

Go past the café to the end of the car park. Then bear left along Gundimore Promenade, or take the lower beach route, where dogs may run free. From the raised path behind the sea wall there are views of **Sandhills** through the mobile homes in the holiday park. Out to sea in 1824 Captain Freemantle (RN) earned the first-ever RNLI Gold Medal for saving the crew of a wrecked Swedish brig. At the end of the promenade you are back at the Quay.

Walk 5: Bargates and Royalty Fishery

Start and finish: Bypass car park next to supermarket, NE end of Fountain Way
Approx. distance: 4 km

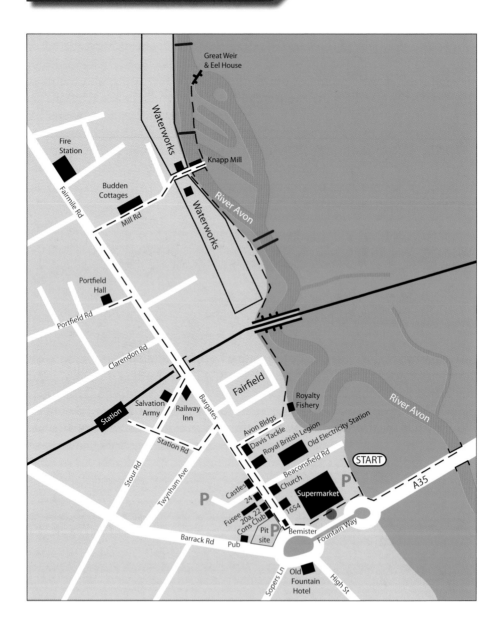

Starting at the east side of the car park furthest from the supermarket, you can look across the **flood plain** of the River Avon. With concrete beneath your feet, modern supermarket behind and rail and road to left and right, you may not realise you are actually standing in one of Christchurch's most ancient sites. (For a better view of the river and flood plain, pop along the footpath/cycleway beside the bypass.)

Make your way out of the car park, turning right around the end of the supermarket in the direction of Bargates. Stay on the upper-level pavement and look for a **blue plaque** on the third brick column along. This records various finds here including Saxon spears, shields and knives, and Neolithic pottery (see photo of the plaque in the Introduction).

At the junction of Fountain Way and Bargates, look right up Bargates and left up the High Street. **Bargates** is named after the north gate that once stood near the top of the High Street. When the bypass was constructed in 1957

it cut Christchurch in two, severing Bargates from the High Street and resulting in the demolition of several buildings, although thankfully not the one-time **Fountain Hotel** – the half-timbered building diagonally across the roundabout, built in 1908, which replaced the Wagon and Horses and was once home to the local newspaper the *Daily Echo* Christchurch district office.

Cross to the small traffic island in Bargates, to the granite **Bemister Fountain**, erected in 1902 in memory of Samuel Bemister, a local gunsmith, bell-hanger and town mayor on seven occasions. The fountain once stood where the roundabout is and quenched the thirst of horses, dogs and people. Note the planting here and on the roundabout. Christchurch is well known for its public flower displays.

Continue across Bargates, so you are alongside **Pit Site** car park. From the name and looking down on it you may deduce that this was once an ancient gravel pit. After that it was a congested slum area, which once had the town stocks in front of an 18th-century lock-up. A great fire in July 1825 destroyed over 50 thatched cottages, hovels, beerhouses and workshops in Pit Site in less than 3 hours. Bear baiting took place here until the sport was outlawed in 1835. The **pub** at the far side of the car park, formerly the Duke of Wellington, was one of the watering holes popular with those stationed at the barracks in Barrack Road.

Walk up Bargates, away from the High Street. The first building on your left is the **Conservative Club** (established 1908). It was originally the home of Thomas Barrow, another local fusee chain maker (1844–51), before becoming a police station in 1851.

The white building further along (**No. 22**, no number displayed) was originally a shop (left) and house (right) where a beer seller, George Dixon, lived. The front of the house was rebuilt and became the home of William Hart (1845–68), owner of the fusee chain factory next-door to the left (**No. 20A**). Note the sign, wall plaque and large windows, which would have given more light to work on the tiny chains.

The last building (**No. 24**) before the road to Bargates car park was **Holm Tree Cottage**, an 18th-century house of cob and thatch when first constructed. The *Christchurch Times* was printed here (1890–1915); the paper was first published in 1855, continuing until 1983.

Continue along the road for **Castles**, everyone's idea of a hardware store, where you can buy almost anything. Castles was previously Home Farm, whose land extended back to Barrack Road.

On the left of the pedestrian crossing is the former **Royalty Inn**, the pub that moved (now redeveloped as housing). Originally called the Red Lion, this was pulled down in 1904/5 as Bargates was widened to accommodate trams, and rebuilt further back from the road. It is said that the concrete base for the tramlines remains under the street. This was the original fishermen's pub, until closure. One unwelcome 'catch' in Bargates in 1936 was a tarantula spider reportedly discovered amongst bananas at a fruiterer in the street.

Continue up Bargates, reaching Twynham Avenue (recalling Christchurch's earlier name). Just up on the right is **Fairfield**, once the site of the field where fairs were held, the final one in 1871. Turn left into Twynham Avenue, then first right into Station Road. Cross over Stour Road to view the **railway station** buildings dating from 1886.

Retrace your steps and leave the station, turning left into Stour Road. The **Salvation Army** was founded by William Booth in East London in 1865 with a mission statement to provide people with a 'hand-up' rather than a 'hand-out'. The church and charity came to Christchurch in 1885, when it used a hall close to the Duke of Wellington pub. The crest on the wall here is the oldest emblem of the Salvation Army, dating to 1879. The band is a fixture at Christmas, playing carols around the Christmas tree in Saxon Square.

At the end of Stour Road, the Victorian **Railway Inn** is on the opposite corner, nowadays frequented by fishermen enjoying the nearby Royalty Fishery.

Turn left across the bridge over the railway, with a view of the station. The **railway line** used to be an anti-tank 'island' in WW2 in case of invasion, and some overgrown **concrete obstacles**, designed to literally stop German tanks in their tracks, may be seen off the other side of the bridge. There is another concrete block at the northern end of the bridge (just before the start of the advertising hoarding and a concrete end-post for a wire-mesh fence).

After the bridge the road becomes Fairmile. Continue on past **Clarendon Road**, named after Edward Hyde, the Earl of Clarendon and Lord of the Manor of Christchurch in the 17th century. Next, turn left into Portfield

Road to admire **Portfield Hall** (just a little way down). The name recalls the field belonging to the town (port) when it was one of the town commons, the largest area of common land at almost 121 ha, with that nearest the Stour available to graze cattle. Little is left of the Portfield due to development, particularly residential, following the Portfield Enclosure Act of July 1873, with Barrack Road Recreation Ground now its last remnant. The Hall is a reminder of Christchurch's military past, the land given to the 57th Battalion Hampshire Regiment in 1908 by Fredrick James Edward Vaughan. It is now a community hall and used by the Sea Cadets.

Go back up to **Fairmile Road**, so named because it was the last mile of road leading to the fair. Cross (using the crossing here). Continue heading

north, then turn right into **Mill Road**, cross over and look for some **plaques** on the three pairs of cottages (Nos 11–21) on the left, dedicated to the **Budden family**, a local family who clearly had means and wanted to do good works.

Continue on, admiring the **mural** and wall painting on the next house. As the road turns to the left, enter the **waterworks** by way of the pedestrian gate,

crossing what used to be the original railway line into Christchurch which closed in 1935. Note the West Hampshire Waterworks buildings dated 1928 and 1937, now part of Bournemouth Water. Inside the 1937 building is an intriguing large glazed dome structure.

Cross over the bridge in front of the brick building **Knapp Mill**, then immediately left alongside the river. Originally there was a Saxon watermill here supplying flour to the town. This burnt down in the 18th century and a new mill was constructed, which ceased trading in 1920 and then caught fire in 1921. The mill buildings were rebuilt as a turbine house in the 1920s and a lease taken by the waterworks to filter water from the Avon and pump it to reservoirs on St Catherine's Hill.

Continue on along the river to reach the **Great Weir**. Standing on the weir you will see an island downstream, either side of which is Edwards Pool (left) and Hayters Pool (right) where two 41¾-lb salmon were caught within a week of each other in 1951. On the weir is the **Eel House**, where eels were caught, and you can see **hatches** (fish ladders), which salmon use to ascend the river.

Return to Knapp Mill, cross back over the bridge and take the footpath to your left, picking up the path alongside the Avon. There is now a pleasant stretch by the river until you reach the current railway line which crosses the Avon on a **metal bridge**. This tranquil spot hides a dark secret for it was around here that Alma Rattenbury took her life on 4 June 1935. Alma had been found not

guilty of the murder of her husband, a retired architect, although her young lover, George Stoner, was sentenced to hang. The murder took place in Bournemouth, where Francis and Alma Rattenbury had their home. Alma calmly took the train from London Waterloo to Christchurch, before walking to these water meadows. As she sat by the riverbank she wrote, 'Oh, to see the swans and spring flowers, and to smell them … it is beautiful here. What a lovely world, really.' In a twist worthy of Shakespeare, Stoner had his sentence commuted to penal servitude (life) and then only served 7 years. On still June evenings the figure of a solitary, silent female figure has been seen sitting in the long grass.

Continue on the path, up to the road called **Avon Buildings** and the entrance to the famous Royalty Fishery. Across the Royalty Fishery car park is a good view of the old **electricity**

The old power station (above) and inside the museum (left). (Courtesy of Christchurch Electricity Museum.)

generating station (1903–26), which provided current for properties in the town and later the tramway and was the model on which other Edwardian power-stations were based. The former Museum of Electricity (closed 2012) has been named a community asset after a campaign by residents and it is hoped that the museum will re-open in the future. Gas arrived in the town 50 years before, the gas works being in Bridge Street.

Walk along Avon Buildings to Bargates. At the main road, the first building on the left is **Davis Tackle**, supplying the needs of fishermen since 1945.

AVON BUILDINGS
LEADING ONLY TO ROYALTY FISHERIES AND PUBLIC FOOTPATH TO RIVER AVON
VERY NARROW CUL · DE · SAC

AVON VALLEY PATH
Salisbury ➡
⬅ Christchurch Priory

A little further on is the **Royal British Legion Club**. The impressive frontage shows that this was once a public cinema, Christchurch's first in 1914. It became the RBLC in 1946.

Pass a gate leading into the former **electricity generating station**. As you cross Beaconsfield Road you come to the **Baptist Church**. First established as a Methodist chapel, the Baptist Church dates to 1874.

Just before reaching Fountain Way is a **set of buildings dating to 1654** on the site of the former Horse and Groom public house, previously the Lugger (*c.* 1800). Joseph Cutler was born here in 1830, making a fortune in the Australian gold rush, then becoming a major benefactor to Bournemouth. A restaurant had the name '1654' at one time, commemorating the date of the building. Turn left at the end of Bargates back to the car park.

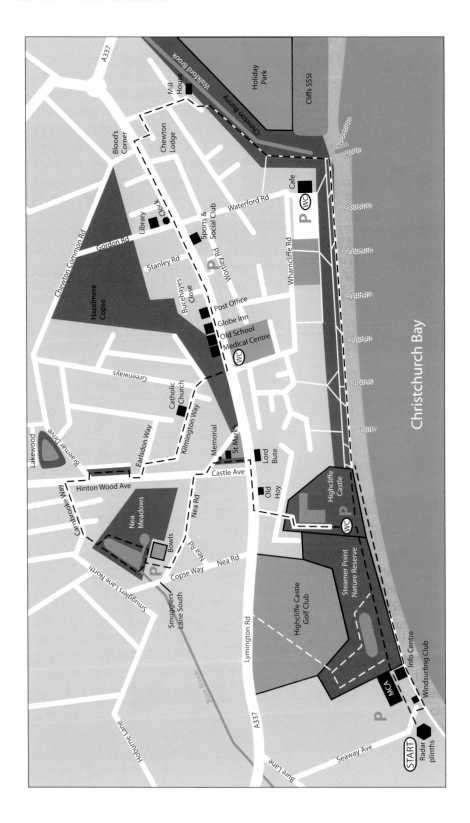

Walk 6:
Highcliffe and Chewton Bunny

Start and finish: Steamer Point car park off Seaway Avenue
Approx. distance: 9 km, or can be shortened to 2 km

From the car park on Friars Cliff, walk towards the cliff-top to the concrete plinth. A **monument and plaque** here record the site's significance in the

early development of radar and satellite communications. The satellite station here was known as RADOME.

Walk back past the car park and through the pedestrian gate into Steamer Point Nature Reserve. On the left is the former **Maritime and Coastguard Agency (MCA) Training Centre**. The MCA implements Government maritime safety policy in the UK, working to prevent loss of life along the coast and at sea. It moved its training operations to a new centre near Fareham in July 2015. **Steamer Point** was acquired by

the MOD in 1939 and radio communications, radar and later satellite were all developed here. 'Golf ball' radar domes were visible on the cliff behind Friars Cliff beach until the late 1960s. The MOD relinquished the site in 1983, when it became a local nature reserve owned by the borough council. There are still **military sentry huts** you will spot on this walk.

The Information Centre here has details of guided walks and events, including practical tasks. Inside, there is an imaginatively painted interpretation wall, with small doors opening to reveal nuggets of nature interest.

Walk through the nature reserve, following signs for Highcliffe Coast Path. At the junction of paths, carry on. Off to the right is a pleasant picnic area and some old tree trunks that have been recycled into seats.

Back on the path, keep on through the gate. Up to the late 1700s this area was known as **Common Gate**, possibly a recollection of a gateway that led to nearby Chewton Common.

After the second gate, turn inland through the car park towards **Highcliffe Castle**. You can explore the 19th-century castle and grounds; there is also a tea room and shop. The magnificent oriel window is a different colour to the surrounding stone as it was taken complete from a medieval house, La Grande Maison in Les Andelys, Normandy.

Follow the drive around the side of the castle, exiting at the main gate. Walk ahead to Lymington Road and turn right. You will come to what is probably Highcliffe's oldest house, the delightfully thatched cottage **The Old Hoy** (right), taking its name from *Isle of Wight Hoy*, a boat that plied between the mainland and the Isle. The Old Hoy was one of three inns in Newtown (Highcliffe's former name) until its licence lapsed in 1868. Hoy House (the Old Hoy's

former name) was in Highcliffe Castle grounds, a smugglers' den by all accounts, then converted from inn to private house by teetotaler Lady Waterford, owner of the castle.

Continue along Lymington Road to the **Lord Bute**. Grade II listed **West Lodge and East Lodge** date from *c.* 1773 and were designed by Robert Adam, architect to George III. These entrance lodges are the only remaining parts of the original stately home here, High Cliff Mansion.

Cross Lymington Road and go through the lych gate to **St Mark's Church**, built in 1843 by Lord Stuart de Rothesay of Highcliffe Castle at his own expense. Follow the gravel path to the side of the churchyard via an avenue of *Ilex* trees (evergreen oak native to the Mediterranean). The solitary bell at the west end of the church

came from St Petersburg. Australian soprano Dame Nellie Melba, a frequent guest at Highcliffe Castle, once sang *Ave Maria* from the balcony in St Mark's.

To the right of the church door, follow the sign for **Selfridge Graves**. Harry Gordon Selfridge (1857–1947) was the founder of Selfridges. His wife Rose died in 1918 and mother Lois Frances in 1924. Selfridge, who rented Highcliffe Castle during WW1, lost his fortune, hence the simplicity of his grave; he died in relative poverty in a flat in Putney. His grave contrasts with the more opulent graves of Lois and Rose. Opposite is the grave of Field Marshal Sir Charles Comyn Egerton, a senior Indian Army officer.

Go back towards the church and walk right alongside the wall. At the first corner, turn right to see the Cameron graves. Lt Col. William Gordon Cameron (1790–1856) lost his sword arm to a cannon ball at Waterloo. His daughter Caroline was the first bride married in St Mark's (1856). The fifth grave along is that of his son Col. Aylmer Spicer Cameron VC (1833–1909). His Victoria Cross was earned during the Indian Mutiny.

Walk back to the gravel path, continuing away from Lymington Road. Reaching Hinton Wood Avenue, you will find the **war memorial**.

Turn left, and go over roads to the crossroads. Cross and proceed ahead down Nea Road. Turn right into Smugglers Lane South, looking for a footpath on the right (after No. 13) taking you into **Nea Meadows**. Nea House, a large 19th-century country house, was demolished in 1940 and some of the land developed as housing, the remainder becoming a nature reserve comprising wildflower meadows, a wildlife pond, central wood and Nea Lake in July 2005.

You now have a choice of route. You can climb the slope beyond the car park, heading left to a **viewpoint**. The **lake** was constructed as a flood defence measure, replacing an original fishing pond. It is fed by both Bure Brook from the north and Chewton Common Drain from the east. Walk along the side of the lake to an information board, which shows pictures of bygone days hay-making and rick-building *c.* 1918.

Alternatively, take the path around the bowling club to the right (far side), crossing the small bridge by the wildlife pond to reach the larger **wildflower meadow**. To your right is a large **tree**, which is obviously good for climbing. Cross the large meadow and take the path around the top of the lake, crossing a small bridge, then following the path to the right and exit the reserve.

Turn right down Carisbrooke Way, then right into Hinton Wood Avenue. Cross and continue along the footpath behind the Wolhayes Garden Estate sign, walking through trees. Reaching the fence, bear right, back to Hinton Wood Avenue. *(Note: if you want to shorten the walk here, continue down Hinton Wood Avenue, then Castle Avenue, bringing you out on Lymington Road close to Highcliffe Castle.)*

Turn left into Earlsdon Way, then immediately right into Kilmington Way. The **Catholic Church of the Holy Redeemer** is further down on the left-hand side.

Reaching Lyme Crescent (right), cut the corner off with the footpath through trees into Greenways. Bear right on another footpath, returning to Lymington Road.

Turn left by the medical centre. On the left is the **Old School House** (the black and white building), with the former caretaker's residence to the left. This was originally a lecture room (1838), then St Mark's

Church School from 1844–1970 (after which the school moved to new buildings in Greenways, close to Chewton Common) and the town library. In the winter of 1907 Kaiser Wilhelm attended a tea party here arranged for the local schoolchildren. Just on from here is the **Globe Inn**, possibly 18th century.

Walking past some shops you come to the Post Office. The plaque on the **letter box** records the town's centenary in 1992; the first car drove through Highcliffe 5 years later in 1897. A relatively new addition to Christchurch, Newtown was the Victorian name, adopted when the area became a popular tourist destination. Prior to Newtown it had been known by the less-flattering name of Slop Pond (a hamlet of thatched cottages, named after a pond on Chewton Common).

Cross Bucehayes Close. At Stanley Road (left) note the attractive **cherub** in a

recess of the wall opposite. Continue along Lymington Road. Opposite is **Highcliffe Sports and Social Club**. In 1887 Lady Waterford, owner of Highcliffe Castle, opened a reading room here, which became a social club in 1903.

Turn left into Gordon Road for the **library**, housed in the former Parish Hall (1906) where Gordon Selfridge entertained children with presents and a tree at Christmas. The library moved here in 1970 from the Old School House. The key to the original door is on the notice board at the back.

Continue along Lymington Road. Next is a **clock and plaque**, the clock curiously mounted on something resembling an upright ski. This clock (1959) replaced one that had been provided to mark the coronation of George V in 1911.

The junction of Lymington Road and Chewton Common Road is known locally as Blood's Corner, after Dr Blood who practiced as a GP in Highcliffe (1930–38). Cross the main road here, taking the footpath to **Chewton Lodge** (road). Turn left, then right into Mill Lane. At the bottom bear right along the footpath to the sea. **Chewton Bunny** was a favourite haunt of smugglers. Ravines were often used to carry contraband inland and this one was heavily wooded so it hid activities. However, there was quicksand at the bottom, which deterred all but the bravest.

Almost immediately left you will see the beautiful **Mill House**, a Grade II listed former water-driven corn mill more than 250 years old, which ceased

operations in 1906. This was once owned by wealthy Dorothy Clutterbuck (1880–1951), a leading member of the New Forest coven, a group of witches. There is also a ghost story concerning the figure of a young man seen in a room in the mill dressed in early-20th-century garb. Famous visitors included Marie Curie, the renowned physicist, who came in the summer of 1912 whilst convalescing following an operation. She stayed here with another eminent female scientist of the day, Hertha Ayrton, who was awarded the Hughes Medal by the Royal Society for groundbreaking work on ripples in sand and water. There was once an older mill here dating back to at least the reign of Elizabeth I.

Continue to the bottom of the ravine via the upper or lower path; both end at the sea, where a large Russian ship was driven ashore in the late 1830s. The sailors were rescued and taken to the Old Hoy. As you emerge onto the grassy slopes you can see how apt a name is Chewton Bunny; this is prime rabbit territory.

You can bear right up the hill to the café and along the cliff-top a short way before descending again, or stay low and turn right along the beach/lower path. (Note: paths may be affected by cliff erosion at times.) Enjoy the view of the Isle of Wight, its proximity causing the phenomenon of four daily tides, which also affects the port of Southampton.

There are various beach/cliff paths for approximately 1.5 km, back to Highcliffe Castle. The easier route back to Steamer Point is up the zig-zag path and back through the nature reserve. However, if you take the more direct sandy beach option there are good views of the cliffs.

Other Walks and Cycling Routes

- The **Stour Valley Way** is a designated footpath, 64 miles (103 km) long, which follows almost all the course of the river, starting at the source at Stourhead (Wiltshire), heading via Wimborne to Christchurch, Mudeford Spit and the sea.
- The **Avon Valley Path** is a 34-mile (55-km) walking route between Salisbury and Christchurch following the River Avon.
- **Christchurch Coastal Path** extends for almost 2.5 miles, from the clifftop at Highcliffe via Highcliffe Castle and Steamer Point Nature Reserve to Mudeford Quay.
- **Mude Valley Greenway** is a traffic-free walking/cycling route from Mudeford Quay through Mude Valley Nature Reserve to Somerford roundabout. It starts at the Haven House Inn on the Quay.
- **Christchurch Millennium Trail** takes you around the town centre, via blue plaques and historic sites. A map of the route is available from Christchurch Information Centre in the High Street.
- **Christchurch Strollers** is a 'walking for health' group, organising walks of around 40 minutes from the likes of Highcliffe Castle (see public information board in the car park), St Catherine's Hill (see entrance to Marsh Lane car park off Fairmile Road) and Saxon Square (meet in the Square).

Christchurch Bicycle Club is a social cycling club with more than 170 members. Christchurch is great for short bike rides to places of interest, or as a start-point for longer rides to the New Forest. Christchurch Council has always been very pro-active towards cycling, with signficant provision for cyclists around the town. This is very commendable for such a tightly built area. Part of the 13,000-mile National Cycle Network, NCN Route 2 passes through Christchurch and there are numerous other cycle routes available.

The website dorsetforyou.com has details on the above walking routes, cycleways and rides, and an interactive map where you can choose your own route, from bridleway and byways to cycle tracks and quiet roads.

Outlying Areas of the Borough

Blackwater

A small hamlet to the north of Christchurch, Blackwater was the site of a rope-ferry crossing over the River Stour. The painting *Blackwater Ferry* by Arthur Henry Davis (1879) is displayed in the Russell Cotes Art Gallery and Museum in Bournemouth. The area is best known today for the Blackwater Junction, a major road junction connecting the dual-carriageway A338 with Christchurch and Hurn (B3073).

Burton

Across the Avon from Christchurch, Burton is a village with a community feel, centred on a village green. Oldest parts date to the early-18th century. St Luke's Church (*c.* 1874) was built by architect Benjamin Ferrey. Edmund Lyons (1790–1858), a Royal Navy commander, was born at Whitehayes House (now flats), and became Baron Lyons of Christchurch in 1856 for service in the Crimea, where he commanded the Black Sea fleet. Local resident Lt-Gen. Bernard Matthew Ward also served in the Crimea (Inkerman and Sevastopol).

Whitehayes House, once the home of Baron Edmund Lyons.

Poet laureate Robert Southey (1774–1843) lived in the village for a couple of years. Preacher John Rickman (1771–1840) wrote a paper suggesting that the government hold a National Census, and as a result he was given the task of preparing the first Census Act, approved by Parliament in 1880. He retired to 'The Cottage' in Burton. Once, whilst sailing between Christchurch and Poole, Rickman was taken by a press gang but fought them

Burton Hall, a fine example of Early-Georgian architecture.

147

off. Burton Hall was built around 1750 as a three-storey private residence, but has since been converted into flats. It is as impressive as any building of that period anywhere in Dorset.

As you drive along the by-pass towards Somerford, you might spot the stump of an old stone cross on the left (about half a mile beyond Stony Lane roundabout), called Staple Cross. Such crosses are usually associated with preaching or a market, and 'staple' can mean a major item of trade or commodity grown or produced in a particular area. As both the Priory and market were so close, however, perhaps 'Staple Cross' was a boundary marker between two or three lordships, from 'stapol' (old English) meaning a stone post or pillar denoting a boundary or meeting place. There would have been more of the cross prior to 1944, when the top was broken by an American tank in the build-up to D-Day.

Fairmile and Jumpers

Jumpers (possibly derived from 'juniper') is a northern extension of Christchurch between Barrack Road and Fairmile Road, which starts at Bargates railway bridge. St George's, Jumpers Road, is a junior church of the Priory. There has been a church here since 1898, although the current one dates from 1928. Fairmile Road is home to Christchurch Fire Station (1948) and Christchurch Hospital (dating to Victorian times).

Community volunteers and the Firefighters charity help support the Fire Station.

Friars Cliff – see Walk 6

Highcliffe – see Walk 6

Hinton

The hamlet of Hinton lies about 3 miles north-east of Christchurch station. St Michael and All Angels Church has a lovely churchyard and Hinton

The Cat and Fiddle, the last port of call for pilgrims and wayfarers before the New Forest, and apparently maintained for this purpose by the Saxon monastery of Christchurch Twynham.

Admiral Station has the feel of a country halt. It was here that Kaiser Wilhelm arrived (from Windsor) with his 50-strong party in November 1907, and the station was frequently used by the Selfridges who used to alight here from Waterloo, before travelling on to Highcliffe Castle. Hinton Admiral House (private) is 18th century with 8 ha of gardens. The Cat and Fiddle is a thatched inn on Lyndhurst Road, once a smugglers' base. The oldest part of the inn was reputedly haunted, but since renovation, reports of any ghostly activity seem to have ceased.

Hurn

Hurn is most famous today for Bournemouth Airport, but it is an ancient village, listed in *Domesday* as 'Herne'. It used to have a railway station until 1935 (now the Avon Causeway pub) and is home to Christchurch Sports Club, where both cricketers and footballers play. A ghostly figure in RAF uniform on a bike was allegedly almost knocked down by a car in 1988, only to disappear (the airport was an RAF station during WW2).

Mudeford – see Walk 4

Purewell – see Walk 2

Somerford

The site of Christchurch Airfield in WW2, there is a plaque at the entrance to Wilverley Road in Somerford recalling the Fleet Air Arm de Havilland Sea Vixen and the aviation history of Christchurch. One hundred and forty-five Sea Vixen interceptors were built here, seeing service with the Royal Navy from 1959–72. The last one left the Christchurch factory in 1962. De Havilland had an aeronautical technical school on Somerford Way, housed in a former theatre, which sadly burned down in 1975. The airfield closed

Part of Christchurch's aviation history, the Sea Vixen (the last one made) used to stand on a plinth at the corner of Wilverley and Somerford Roads. She is now being looked after by Tangmere Museum of Military Aviation. (© Hampshire County Council. Provided by Hampshire Cultural Trust.)

in 1964 and the factory in 1966, with the loss of 2000 jobs. Cecil Gardner's factory on Somerford Road (which closed in the early 1990s) made electrical components such as transformers, but also top-secret components for the bouncing bomb.

Somerford Grange was home to Christchurch's final prior, John Draper, who died there in 1552, the building surviving until 1935, when it made way for the airfield. Several car drivers have reported seeing a hooded figure (Draper?) in the vicinity.

Sopley

Another village listed in *Domesday*, Sopley lies north of Burton and Winkton on the old Christchurch to Ringwood road and is just outside the New Forest National Park. Most buildings are 19th century, although the prominent Woolpack Inn dates to 1725, when it was a cottage with wool store, becoming a pub in 1783.

Stanpit – see Walk 2

Tuckton

Tuckton is, strictly speaking, across the water (Stour) in Bournemouth but is included here because of its closeness and unusual stories. Russian spy Melita Norwood, the most important female agent recruited by the Soviets, was born in Bournemouth and had connections with Tuckton. The Russian link goes back further, as in Tsarist days there was a Russian aristocratic 'colony' in Tuckton, including a daughter-in-law of Tolstoy, exiled for opposition to Tsarist oppression. The Russians were sometimes seen in Christchurch.

Walkford

Amberwood Inn – former coach house turned pub.

Between Hinton and Highcliffe, Walkford dates to the 19th century. Former Amberwood House (in Amberwood Gardens) has been converted to apartments, but its coach house is still there on the main road, albeit now as a pub.

Winkton

A small hamlet betwixt Burton and Sopley, Winkton has a pair of fine buildings: Winkton House built close to the Avon, formerly with fisheries and ice house, and Georgian Winkton Lodge across the road, which was until recently Homefield School. Winkton Lodge was the start point for the procession to honour Christchurch's greatest hero, Admiral Lyons, on his successful return from the Crimea, which took him to Humby's (the Kings Arms) in January 1856, 5 months before he was raised to the peerage

as Baron Lyons. It must have been quite a thing for a small town like Christchurch to have had such a military hero in its midst. Winkton Lodge was also the home of Admiral John Edward Walcott, MP for Christchurch for four parliaments (1859–68), who gifted the town its Town Hall at Saxon Square, re-erected there in 1860.

Winkton Lodge, a fine place to start a procession.

Help and Information

Maps

The general area is covered by OS Explorer Map OL22 and Landranger 195. A detailed map of the town is available from the Christchurch Information Centre.

Transport

Wilts & Dorset (0845 0727 093) and Yellow **buses** (01202 636110) operate frequent services to and from Christchurch High Street. **Trains** leave from the station in Stour Road (off Bargates), which is 5 minutes' walk from the High Street. There are two trains an hour from London (Waterloo), including a semi-fast service; however, the fastest trains do not stop at Christchurch. There is also a service to Bournemouth, Poole, Dorchester and Weymouth. **Ferries** from Town Quay take passengers to Hengistbury Head and Tuckton. **Taxis** pick up at Christchurch station and Bargates (close to Fountain Way).

Christchurch Information Centre

49 High Street, tel 01202 499199, www.visit-dorset.com/tourist-information-centres/christchurch-information-centre-p652723
Open 6 days a week: Mon 9 am–4.30 pm, Tues–Sat 10 am–4.30 pm.

Museums

Red House Museum
Quay Road, tel 0845 6025635 or 01202 482860,
http://www3.hants.gov.uk/redhouse
Open Tues–Fri 10 am–5 pm, Sat 10 am–4 pm, admission free

Visitors can enjoy displays of local and social history, as well as temporary exhibitions (there is always something new to see). There is a permanent display of furniture by renowned designer Romney Green, who had a workshop at 3 Bridge Street, including a room setting *c.* 1935. Green, a noted craftsman, sailor and poet, died in 1945, aged 74, when his bicycle was in collision with a motor-coach at the Barrack Road–Stour Road crossing. A visit wouldn't be complete without spending time in the gardens overlooked by the Priory, where it is possible to enjoy refreshments. The Local Studies Resource Room on the first floor includes an extensive photographic collection from Victorian times to the present. Friends of the Red House was established in 1951and today has around 200 members, providing volunteers, as well as running a programme of lectures and fundraising activities.

Bournemouth Aviation Museum
Merritown Lane, Hurn, tel 01202 473141, www.aviation-museum. co.uk
See website for opening times; there is an admission charge

Providing a hands-on experience for people interested in aviation, exhibits include over a dozen aircraft, including a Westland Wessex helicopter where you can sit in the cockpit. The museum is opposite the airport and has an elevated viewing area.

Christchurch Library

Druitt Buildings, High Street, tel 01202 485938, www.dorsetforyou.com/ christchurchlibrary
Open Mon–Sat (closes 1 pm Wed)

The library was extended in 2013 and visitors can now enjoy improved facilities from a 60% increase in space.

Lifeguards

RNLI beach lifeguards are on hand during the summer. Mike Winter is an area supervisor, with 25 staff reporting to him.

'We have one of the youngest teams we've ever had, with four under-18s, which is only possible because of the work of the Christchurch Lifesaving Club, which

trains them from a young age. They come to us with a good grounding, which we can build on with our own high-level training and well-tested operating procedures.

Christchurch is divided into three units, Avon Beach, Highcliffe and Friars Cliff, with two lifeguards manning each station. Our service is 95% preventative and we feel that we provide a good service through Lifeguard patrols, prevention, education and signage. When something does happen, our lifeguards are all highly trained to deal with a range of incidents and react accordingly.'

Other Useful Contacts and Sources of Information

www.visitchristchurch.info
Christchurch Community Partnership – tel 01202 989632,
    www.christchurchcommunitypartnership.org.uk
The Priory – tel 01202 485804, www.christchurchpriory.org
Christchurch Sailing Club – tel 01202 483150,
    www.christchurchsailingclub.co.uk
Highcliffe Castle – tel 01425 278807, www.highcliffecastle.co.uk
Regent Centre – tel 01202 499199, www.regentcentre.co.uk

Bibliography

Andrew IC (1998) *Lord Lyons of Christchurch*. Christchurch Local History Society.

Andrew IC (2000) *Salisbury Road, Burton*. Christchurch Local History Society.

Ashley H (1985) *Explore Dorset*. Countryside Books, Newbury.

Barker J (1993) *Christchurch Barracks*. Bournemouth Local Studies Publications.

Christchurch Official Guide (1960). Christchurch and District Chamber of Trade.

Christchurch Walkabout. Christchurch Writers' Circle.

Cockain E (2004) *The Saxon Face of Christchurch Priory*. Natula Publications, Christchurch.

Cockain E (2008) *Christ's Church, a DIY Guide to Detecting Antiquity*. Natula Publications, Christchurch.

Crow R (1987) *The Priory Church Christchurch – Outline Guide for the Use of Guides and Stewards*. Christchurch Priory Pilgrims and Tourism Committee.

Eels D (2008) *The Medieval Markets & Fairs of Christchurch*. Christchurch Antiquarians.

Franklin R (2008) *Admiral Jackson of Verno Christchurch 1787–1876*. Natula Publications, Christchurch.

Guttridge R (1986) *Dorset Murders*. Roy Gasson Associates, Wimborne.

Herringshaw SD (1981) *A Portrait of Highcliffe*. Natula Publications, Christchurch.

Historic Christchurch Book 1 (1995). Christchurch Local History Society.

Historic Christchurch Book 2 (1998). Christchurch Local History Society.

Hodges MA (1978) *Prepared for Battle*. Christchurch Printing Co.

Hodges MA (2001) *Christchurch – A Photographic History of Your Town*. Black Horse Books, Salisbury.

Hodges MA (2002) *Ghosts of Christchurch Hundred*. Natula Publications, Christchurch.

Hodges MA (2003) *Christchurch Castle – A Short History*. Natula Publications, Christchurch.

Hodges MA (2003) *Christchurch – The Golden Years*. Dorset Books, Tiverton.

Hodges MA (2005) *St Catherine's Hill – A Short History*. Natula Publications, Christchurch.

Hodges MA (2008) *Christchurch – A Brief History*. Christchurch Local History Society.

Hoodless WA (2010) *Christchurch Curiosities*. The History Press, Stroud.

Needham J (2013) *Christchurch Then & Now in Colour*. The History Press, Stroud.

Newman S (1998) *Images of England, Christchurch*. Tempus Publishing, Stroud.

Newman S (2000) *The Christchurch and Bournemouth Union Workhouse*. Published by Sue Newman.

Newman S (2009) *Christchurch Through Time*. Amberley Publishing, Stroud.

Newman S & Tizzard M (2007) *The Christchurch Commons*. Natula Publications, Christchurch.

Osborn G (1986) *Dorset Curiosities*. Dovecote Press, Wimborne.

Powell M (1993) *1784 – The Battle of Mudeford*. Natula Publications, Christchurch.

Powell M (1995) *Christchurch Harbour*. Natula Publications, Christchurch.

Samuel OJ (1983) *Hoburne Bygone Days*. Published by Olive J. Samuel.

Samuel OJ (1985) *Bure Homage Mudeford – The History of a Mansion and Estate by the Sea*. Published by Olive J. Samuel.

Samuel OJ (2001) *The Ancient Estate of Nea, Highcliffe*. Natula Publications, Christchurch.

Samuel OJ (2003) *The Anchorage – Seaside Retreat*. Natula Publications, Christchurch.

Stannard M (1999) *The Makers of Christchurch: A Thousand Year Story*. Natula Publications, Christchurch.

Stevens D (2011) *From the Archives*. Arbentin Books, Christchurch.

Stevenson I (2008) *Highcliffe Castle Guide Book*. Christchurch Borough Council.

Tate P (2012) *A Walk Along Convent Walk*. Avon Garde, Christchurch.

Tate P (2013) *On the Trail of the Christchurch Dragon*. Avon Garde, Christchurch.

Underwood P (1988) *Ghosts of Dorset*. Bossiney Books, Launceston.

White A (1967) *The Chain Makers*. Red House Museum and Christchurch Local History Society.

White A (1974) *The Mudeford and Stanpit Handbook* (updated and reissued 2004). Published by Allen White.

White A (1982) *Christchurch High Street Through the Years*. Published by Allen White.

White A (1986) *Christchurch Through the Years – Bargates, Fairmile and Barrack Road* (updated and reissued 2011). Published by Allen White.

White A (2003) *Christchurch Through the Years – Bridge Street & Purewell*, 2nd edn. Red House Museum, Christchurch.

Wood C (2009) *75th Anniversary 1934–2009. Souvenir Booklet Celebrating 75 Years of Sailings by the Vintage Headland Boats on Christchurch Harbour*.

Woodhead L (2007) *Shopping, Seduction & Mr Selfridge*. Profile Books, London.

Young JA (1984) *The Ringwood Christchurch and Bournemouth Railway*. Bournemouth Local Studies Publications.

About the Author

Steve Roberts was born in Worcester in 1957 and brought up and educated in the Vale of Evesham. He completed teacher training in Birmingham, then taught in Brighton, Southend and Uxbridge, before moving to Bournemouth and marrying Val in 1984. He worked in IT for many years, becoming a project manager and Chartered Insurer. He set himself up as a freelance writer, public speaker and private tutor in 2012, and has had non-fiction articles published in over 50 different magazines. *Lesser Known Christchurch* is his first book.

www.steveroberts.org.uk
Twitter: @SRChristchurch

Other books by Roving Press

If you enjoyed this book, why not try others in the Lesser Known series?

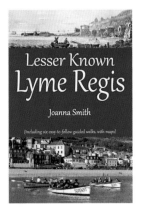 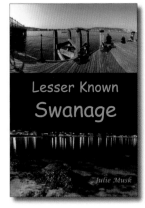 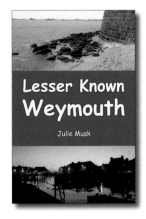

Want a different perspective and closer look? Rather like having your own personal guide, these books offer a close-up, contemporary view of the past and present.

Quotes from local people give a unique insight and they are packed with surprising 'lesser known' facts and stories.

With walks suitable for all ages, be inspired to explore these places and see what many visitors, and even residents, often miss.

Roving
Press

www.rovingpress.co.uk
If you like exploring, you'll love our books

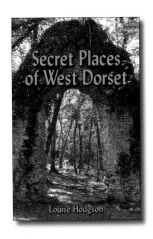

Secret Places of West Dorset
Louise Hodgson

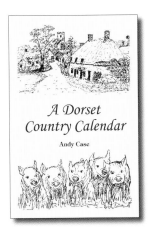

A Dorset Country Calendar
Andy Case

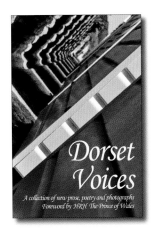

Dorset Voices
A collection of new prose, poetry and photographs
Foreword by HRH The Prince of Wales

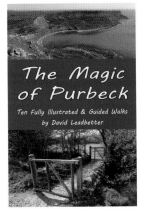

The Magic of Purbeck
Ten Fully Illustrated & Guided Walks
by David Leadbetter

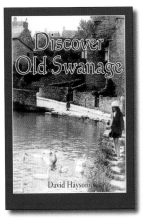

Discover Old Swanage
David Haysom

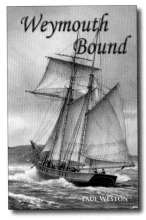

Weymouth Bound
PAUL WESTON

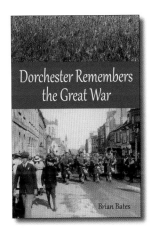

Dorchester Remembers the Great War
Brian Bates

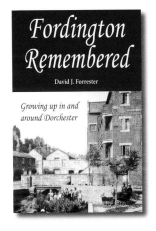

Fordington Remembered
David J. Forrester
Growing up in and around Dorchester

The SPIRIT OF PORTLAND
Revelations of a Sacred Isle
Gary Biltcliffe

Index